Hope

Hope

My Life in Football

By Hope Powell
With Marvin Close

BLOOMSBURY
LONDON · OXFORD · NEW YORK · NEW DELHI · SYDNEY

Bloomsbury Sport
An imprint of Bloomsbury Publishing Plc

50 Bedford Square
London
WC1B 3DP
UK

1385 Broadway
New York
NY 10018
USA

www.bloomsbury.com

BLOOMSBURY and the Diana logo are trademarks of
Bloomsbury Publishing Plc

First published 2016

© Hope Powell, 2016

British Library Cataloguing-in-Publication Data
A catalogue record for this book is available from the British Library.

Library of Congress Cataloguing-in-Publication data has been applied for.

ISBN: HB: 978-1-4729-2556-5
ePub: 978-1-4729-2558-9

2 4 6 8 10 9 7 5 3 1

Typeset in Adobe Garamond Pro by Deanta Global Publishing Services,
Chennai, India
Printed and bound in Great Britain by CPI Group (UK) Ltd, Croydon CR0 4YY

To find out more about our authors and books visit www.bloomsbury.com.
Here you will find extracts, author interviews, details of forthcoming events
and the option to sign up for our newsletters.

Contents

Introduction

'The game of football is quite unsuitable for females and ought not to be encouraged' – the Football Association, 1921

I was born in 1966, the year England won the World Cup. It's hard to believe, but at the time I came into this world women were banned by the FA from playing football in this country.

For 50 years, the oldest football association in the world did not recognise women's football, did not approve of it and refused to let it happen on any pitch, patch of ground or stadium that had any association with the FA. They gave the red card to any qualified match official officiating women's games. They banned recognised coaches and managers from working with women's teams.

Before I tell you about my life, it's really important to understand this because it's one of the major reasons why women's football has had to fight so hard for recognition in this country. Most of the world has had a long head start on us, because our national association denied women the right to play the greatest game. I am a genuine student of that game and always want to learn. One of the things that has fascinated me is learning more about the history of women's football in the United Kingdom. This is what I know.

Women were playing organised football in this country well before the outbreak of World War One. But it was during the

Great War when women's football really took off. With the men away, women came much more into the workplace. Thousands got jobs in the armaments factories, which were dangerous places to work – not just because of accidents and explosions, but due to the chemicals that were used in the making of bombs and bullets. To try to give the women a healthier workplace, they were encouraged to get out during their breaks, exercise and play sport. The game the girls all wanted to play was football.

Armaments factories all had their own teams, and matches began between them to help raise money for war charities. Gradually, the women became more skilled. Professional male footballers invalided out of the war came home to coach and train them. Standards rose, games grew to be ever more competitive, and women's football became a big deal up and down the country. A nationwide tournament, the Munitionettes' Cup, was launched. Matches were played at Old Trafford, Ewood Park, Highbury and many other professional club grounds, in front of crowds numbering 20,000 and 30,000. Women's football developed from being a novelty to serious sporting business.

Then the war ended. The men came home and were given their jobs back in the armaments factories. Most of the women lost work and many of the factory teams folded. But the keenest of the women players were determined to play on. New clubs were formed, one of which became legendary – the Dick, Kerr's Ladies team. Based in the north-west, the side attracted the country's best women players. They played, and beat, a French women's national team and, in 1920, played a match at Goodison Park against St Helen's in front of 53,000 paying fans.

But a powerful lobby against women's football had begun – and the FA listened to it. In 1921, the FA effectively banned women from playing football in this country, a decision that would not be changed for 50 years. It's probably one of this country's biggest sporting injustices, but sadly unknown by many and largely forgotten.

The FA made much of a book published in 1920 by Dr Arabella Kenealy, entitled 'Feminism and Sex-Extinction'. Dr Kenealy did womankind a huge disservice. Her book gravely warned that 'over-use, in sports and games, of the muscles of shoulder and chest, occasions atrophy of mammary glands ... such sterilisation, where it is not actually producing diseased and degenerate offspring, is producing a pitiful race of pallid and enfeebled babies and children.'

The FA pounced upon her warning, gave it maximum publicity through the press, and went out of its way to smother women's football in the cot. They even lectured other countries on the ills of the game. When the Dick, Kerr's Ladies went on tour to Canada, the FA wrote to their male Canadian counterparts urging them to ban the team from playing in their country. The Canadian FA agreed and the Dick, Kerr's Ladies were forced to travel south to the USA to rearrange their tour to play against American teams. Even then, the US football authorities would only let them compete against men's teams. Rather interestingly, in their six matches, they won two, drew two and lost two.

For over 50 years, the women's game in England went 'underground'. Matches were played on rugby grounds and in parks, but mostly not in any kind of organised way. There were no leagues, no structures and little administration.

In 1969, the fightback began. The England men's World Cup win in 1966 was a real shot in the arm for English football generally. Everyone wanted to play. The rebel Women's Football

Association was formed and, though it was a terminally underfunded and largely voluntary organisation, it sowed the seeds of what was to come. In 1971, thanks to pressure from UEFA, the all-male board at the FA was forced to lift its ban on women's football being played on their affiliated grounds. Not that this meant they would have the remotest interest in becoming involved in supporting the women's game.

The WFA battled on, and in the same year launched the first national knockout Cup for women, the Mitre Trophy, which would eventually become the FA Women's Cup. A year later, the WFA launched an official England national team – almost a hundred years after the first men's international fixture. Their first match was a 3–2 win against Scotland in Greenock. Sylvia Gore had the honour of scoring England's first ever international goal.

In 1975 the Sex Discrimination Act was made law, a long overdue and genuine step forward for gender equality in Britain generally. But football was exempted. Those responsible for framing the Act argued that women had many qualities superior to those of men, but did not have the strength or stamina to run, to kick and tackle.

So as late as 1975, the establishment officially viewed women as poor, weak little things who shouldn't be let near a football. It was against this background that I began to play football. All I ever wanted to do in my life was to play the game and to fight the cause for women's football. This is my story.

Chapter 1

London in the Seventies

When I was seven I started to go down to the British Oxygen cage on Harriott Close. At one time they'd stored cylinders of gas there, but when I was a kid it hadn't been used for that for years. It was where all the boys on my council estate in Greenwich, south London, used to go to play football. The chain-link fences were a good ten feet high and the playing surface was concrete. Sometimes there would be dozens of kids in there kicking a ball about. Other times, they'd play a game and pick two teams from all the available kids. Those who weren't picked would become the crowd.

To begin with, I never got picked because I was a girl. The only girl. Then one day they picked me and wished they hadn't. I was little but was already better than all the boys there. I had superior ball control, could beat a man, pass a ball. From as long ago as I can remember, it all came naturally. I was always better than all of the boys in the cage. It was easy. Sport was always natural to me.

All I ever wanted to do was to be a footballer. I had pictures of Kevin Keegan and Ray Wilkins on my bedroom wall. Keegan, because he was the player of the moment when I was a kid. I related to him so much because he was all energy, industry, and though not the most naturally gifted player in the world, he seemed to work so hard at his game and always go that extra mile. Ray Wilkins, because he had nice legs.

I followed Liverpool because of Keegan. But I supported Arsenal because, at the time, they were the best club in London and I am a Londoner through and through. Those were the days of the gloriously flamboyant Charlie George, the no-nonsense George Graham and Frank McLintock and the legendary and lovely Bob Wilson. In 1971, they won the league and Cup double and had a team packed full with international players.

I used to watch *Match of the Day* on TV, study what the players were doing and then go out into the cage and try to copy their skills. I'd watch how they'd trap and control a ball; how they'd make decisions about when to send over a cross, direct a pass, beat a man or take on a player. I soaked it all up, and then for the rest of the week would try to replicate what I'd seen and analysed in my young mind.

My first major injury was caused not in a football match, but came about because of my love of football. I was eight or nine years of age and had been banned from playing out. I can't remember why, but I do recall that I was made to sit with my red maths tables books and learn my times tables over and over again. I gazed out of my bedroom window and saw all my friends playing football outside. I was so desperate to take part in the nightly kickabout, I jumped out of my bedroom window like Superwoman, but landed like Blundergirl. I got splattered on the grass below, broke my leg and blacked out.

My true road to Damascus moment was the 1978 World Cup in Argentina. I'd come home from school, and because of the time difference, the matches would start at about four o'clock in the afternoon. It was my first true footballing masterclass. I remember wondering why the England team weren't there, but after hanging on to every word the summarisers were saying, realised that beyond the club football I knew about, England were not good.

We might have won the World Cup in the year of my birth, but I would soon learn that the seventies was an odd decade for England. English club sides dominated Europe, with the likes of Liverpool, Nottingham Forest and Aston Villa among the domestic sides who won eight European titles throughout the seventies and early eighties. Yet our national side was poor. The World Cup-winning squad, many of whom had gone on to perform brilliantly in Mexico 1970, had largely been replaced by lesser lights. Not only didn't we make it to the 1978 World Cup finals, we hadn't qualified for 1974 either.

But there was always Scotland – a team full of players who I knew about, many of whom played in the Football League. They were my first point of connection to something I could understand about the exotic, carnival-like atmosphere that surrounded the games I was watching. Once I'd got connected, I began to drink in the unbelievable talents of players like Mario Kempes, Rob Rensenbrink, Karl-Heinz Rummenigge and Johnny Rep. I was blown away by Archie Gemmill's wonder goal against the Netherlands, and willed Scotland to win. But the team I enjoyed the most was Peru. They were eliminated in the final group stage, but played with a joy and a swagger that kept me glued to our old black and white telly. Their star was centre-forward Teófilo Cubillas, who was big, strong and skilful. He scored twice against Scotland in Peru's 3–1 group win and then hit a hat-trick in their 4–1 win over Iran. I loved Peru's strip: the white shirt with a red diagonal stripe. I loved the fact that until the World Cup, I knew nothing about Peru or where it was. Suddenly, they were my 'new team'. I loved watching the football. But I also loved the fact that watching 'my' Peru and the World Cup made my little world on a council estate in south London feel a whole lot bigger.

Over 20 years later I would get to work with my early hero Teófilo during the 2008 Beijing Olympics. We'd both been sent by FIFA to do a technical study on the male and female football teams in the tournament. Sometimes you meet your heroes and are disappointed. Not in this case. Teófilo was a lovely man.

What I also realised about the 1978 World Cup, which may seem bizarre now, was that there were no female footballers playing in the matches. It had just never occurred to me before that it was only men. But I didn't care. I was convinced that one day I would earn my living being a footballer. Today, I can't quite believe my naivety. My world was so small, pretty much confined to our housing estate.

As a kid, I hardly went anywhere – not even into central London much, never mind anywhere else in the UK. Nowhere, really, until I was ten years old, when I had the adventure of a lifetime, flying to Jamaica to meet members of my extended family. It was an experience that still has an effect upon me to this day.

My mum, my brother Brian, my cousin Angie and I travelled on Christmas Day, 1976, and after a long flight took a taxi out to an area called Bull Savannah, St Elizabeth Parish, on Jamaica's south coast. It's where my mum's family come from – she's the youngest of nine brothers and sisters. My dad was one of eight. So I had plenty of relatives out there. It could not have been more different from our life in south London. Bull Savannah was a copper mining area. The people from there are light-skinned, like me. Jamaicans called us the red people, because everyone was covered with this red dirt and dust. There was no running water, no flushing toilets. My mum's family were quite poor. They had to draw water from a big tank. There was no electricity and, at night, you had to carry little oil lamps around. But my entire memory of it was that life there was fun. No one wore shoes, everyone was free. My young cousins, uncles, aunts and great-aunts and uncles all lived in the moment. Everyone talked and interacted together – old and young people, different generations.

They buried members of their family on their own plots of land, so you'd be sat having breakfast on your grandfather's tomb. They didn't have toys or televisions. They'd milk the goats, cultivate the land and learn to be resourceful. You'd cook in a big pot for everyone; everything was very communal. No matter what little they had, everyone rubbed along together and shared what they had. As a young kid, this had a long-lasting effect upon me. Loyalty to family and friends is hugely important to me, and my beliefs about that very much go back to my time in Bull Savannah.

Although I probably only subconsciously realised it at the time, being there also taught me a lot about self-reliance. You didn't get given anything on a plate. To live and survive, you had to sort everything out for yourself and those that you were with. There was a resilience and a mentality about my extended family that had a massive influence upon the young me. If I was going to get on in life – and get the life I wanted – I knew I would have to fight and scrap for it. I was already getting an awareness of that growing up in south London, anyway. But this trip to Jamaica really brought it home.

I learnt some bizarre things about my family. In Jamaica, everyone has a nickname. What I soon discovered was that my mum, whose real name was Linever, was known out there as 'Little Mac'. My uncle's name was Odlin, but everyone called him

'Frank'. A cousin I'd known all my life as 'Evert' was born with the name Octavius. My birth father left us when I was tiny and we hardly knew one another. Years later, I organised his funeral and went with my cousin to sign his death certificate. Everyone had called him 'Veron', my mum included. But I discovered through his death certificate that his real name was Vernon. Not even Mum knew that.

My mum was very ill while we were in Jamaica. A couple of weeks before we'd flown out she'd had an operation to remove her thyroid and had had to have a blood transfusion. Once we were there she became dangerously anaemic and, as we were preparing to fly back, she sat in the departure lounge drifting in and out of consciousness. She basically had to be taken off the plane because she was so ill. I remember screaming the place down, shouting and crying for my mum. It was utterly traumatic for Brian and me as young children. The air hostesses looked after us on the trip home. They were lovely. But it was a nightmare to watch my mum being carried off the plane. We didn't know it at the time, but she nearly died while we were flying home across the Atlantic. She had to have a series of blood transfusions in Jamaica, and they wouldn't let her fly home for another three weeks. When we got home to south London, the rest of my family looked after us.

Like a lot of people's, my family background is a complex one. As I said, my birth father left Mum, my elder brother Brian and myself when I was a toddler. I have very little memory of him, but family members have told me through the years that he was a bully and a drunk who used to knock Mum about. As a child, I had virtually no contact with him except for one accidental meeting in Deptford Market when I was about nine or ten. I was shopping with my mum and we bumped into him and his new partner – and their three girls. Apparently, I had three stepsisters. Strangely, and I don't know whether it was through guilt or regret, he'd called one of them Lin, after my mum. We were never in contact again, until years later when my father died.

When I was little, Mum got a new partner, Carl. He had two sons, Terry and Steve, and a daughter called June. Eventually we all moved in together. We left our estate in Peckham, where I was born, to live on a new estate in Greenwich. Mum and Carl had bought our new house for £11,000 – four bedrooms, a garage and a garden. It was a safer estate than Peckham, but we still had our moments. It was mainly white families, with a few black families. Sometimes we used to get cat- and dogshit left on our doorstep, as well as the odd bit of abuse from a few local white residents. But most people rubbed along pretty well together, regardless of their colour.

My memory is that, at the beginning, everything worked out OK. I was the youngest of the five kids in the house, got on fine with Terry and Steve, and I really took to my stepsister June. We used to share a room together, and talk and giggle under our sheets until late into the night.

Life at home was strict. I was quite scared of my mum, but I was also very strong-willed. West Indian culture was very much: 'Boys do this, girls do that.' We girls had chores to do in the house. I was very militant and refused to do mine, unless my big brother Brian did some too. It just didn't seem fair. So, in the end, we had him regularly doing the washing-up.

I fought most with Brian. We used to scrap like cats and dogs, and he used to bully me. But, throughout my adult life, he's grown to become one of my closest and most trusted friends. In many ways, we became close because of Carl.

When I was younger, my relationship with Carl was OK. He was a mechanic and a very practical man. He once made a bike for us kids from scratch, getting a frame here, wheels and gears there, and, basically, he built this incredible bicycle. But as time went by, and I grew older and more aware of what was happening in the house, I came to loathe and despise Carl. Carl was clever with his hands, but brutal with his fists. I began to see he was a bully too, just like my birth father. He would verbally slag Mum off, constantly criticise her and eat away at her self-confidence. Carl was a big, strong, muscular guy and, as I became eight or nine, I realised that he was knocking her around. My mum, bless her, tried to keep it away from the kids as much as she possibly could. But as soon as I realised what was going on, I would make it my business to put myself between Carl and Mum if he tried to have a go at her. Even though I was just a scrawny little kid and he was a big powerful man.

Carl was always on a hair trigger and we were never sure what kind of mood he would come back to the house in. Life in the home became darker, with everyone looking for signs of potential blow-ups, always trying to read his unpredictable moods. I'd often stay awake at night, listening out for tell-tale noises, shouting and rows. I found it increasingly hard to sleep, worrying about what might happen next.

My little gang of friends at Annandale Primary School on our estate provided a blessed release from the darkness of Carl. Gary Denny was my first boyfriend. We used to fold our arms together and hold hands under the desk. I still know him now. On my estate, my friends were like a big extended family. There was Paul Attard, whose family were from Malta; my next-door neighbour, Rina Dunning; and my best friend, Patrick Finch. Patrick's mum and dad were always really kind to me, and I think they must have trusted me above all the other kids. They used to say to Patrick, 'When Hope goes in, that's when you come home.' Paul's brother Frank was the first person I knew who played with a professional club. He was on the books of Charlton Athletic, but didn't make it in the end.

All the gang were sports mad, and if we weren't playing football, we'd be shooting pool and playing table tennis down at the local youth club. That's pretty much all there was to do on the estate. But, on the odd occasion, people did let their hair down together. In 1977, when it was the Queen's Silver Jubilee, we had a really big street party. There were tables out on the road full of food everyone had brought out, and a sound system playing Top 30 hits. Someone put on an old version of 'Brown Girl In The Ring'. Everyone was shouting for me to get 'in the ring' and dance, because I was the only 'brown girl' there. I wasn't impressed.

There were street fights we used to get involved in, but little of that was racial. It was basically territorial. I remember a fight we had that was our school versus another nearby school. It was a mass scrap. I remember physically kicking and thumping these kids, boys and girls, trying to beat the shit out of them. In hindsight, that doesn't sound pretty, but it's what you did to fit in and be a part of your 'people'.

One day, June and my two half-brothers just weren't there any more. They'd moved out to live with their birth mother. They were there one minute and then they were gone. There was no discussion about it in the house, no explanation as to why. What it did mean was that Carl got meaner, and I was starting to get increasingly worried for my mum. I so much hated having Carl in the house, for everything that he did and everything that he was,

I virtually stopped talking to him. I grew to utterly despise Carl. He was a monster who was hurting my mum.

I made sure I got plenty of time alone with her. I used to really enjoy sitting in front of the telly snuggled up together on the sofa. She used to love boxing, and we'd watch all the Ali, Frazier and Foreman fights. In those days, it was rare to see black faces on British TV, and those guys were winners, fighters, showing the world what black people could do.

Perhaps bizarrely, one of Mum's and my favourite TV programmes is now regarded by some as one of the most racist to ever appear on British TV, a sitcom called *Love Thy Neighbour*. The show featured a white racist and his wife who lived next door to a black family. As I say, it was rare to see black faces on TV so Mum and I used to love watching, because it always showed the black couple to be far smarter and far more thoughtful than the stupid white racist. I always hoped that that was what the writers of the show were trying to achieve, but it sure did get a lot of seriously bad press in the ensuing years. In truth, it was a product of its time, so I'm not surprised that it's never shown on TV today. Thankfully, attitudes have moved on.

There was always a lot of music in the house. My mum loved musicals and we'd sit and watch things like *West Side Story* and *Hello, Dolly!* She was absolutely mad about Elvis, and his records were always playing. When he died, Mum was distraught – I remember it was like our house was in mourning. I couldn't afford to buy records very often, so like a lot of people at the time I used to tape the Top 40 off Radio 1.

But like today, I didn't do much else other than eat, drink and live football. I went to Abbey Wood School in 1977 when I was 11, and found out that there was another girl playing the game too. Her name was Jane Bartley. We would become great friends and ended up playing together for Millwall. We both became internationals, me for England, Jane for Wales. At Abbey Wood, we turned out for the school team – for a while.

One day, we played – and beat – a nearby school. Some of their teachers and parents kicked up a fuss about two girls being in the Abbey Wood team. They were just fed up they'd got beat, but decided to take it further. The school complained to the powers that be, and Jane and I were banned from playing mixed football with the boys. The supreme irony was that the people who banned us were the FA – my first brush with an organisation I would later serve for so many years.

The case became quite a local cause célèbre and appeared in all the south London newspapers. Our head of PE, Mr Morland, took up our case and then appealed, unsuccessfully, against the decision. I'm not sure whether it was because he was sticking up for the right of girls to play mixed football, or fed up that he'd lost his best two school-team players.

But that wasn't to be the end of it. Three years later, our head, Christine Whatford, wrote to the Equal Opportunities Commission to try to have the ban overturned. But still no joy. It was a load of old nonsense. At the time, Jane and I had just made our debuts for our respective countries, but we weren't allowed to play football for our school team.

I have a lot of fond memories of Abbey Wood School. When I made my England debut, the staff painted a portrait of me on a school wall, holding my England cap. It was next to a painting of the snooker star Steve Davis, who had been at Abbey Wood some years before me. But getting banned from playing for the school was a real blow. Although as I got to know Jane better, I discovered that she was playing for a youth team at Millwall Lionesses. This was amazing and inspiring news for me – that girls were playing organised football in teams together. What I would also learn was that Millwall were one of the oldest clubs in women's football, and pioneers in the game. Founded in 1971, they became the first club in the country to open a Girls Centre of Excellence, to help develop young footballers from the age of eight right up to senior level.

When it was formed, Millwall FC was trying to shake off a terrible image for hooliganism and racism. When I was growing up in the seventies, English football in general had a real problem with boot boys and thugs, who'd travel the country to fight one another at matches. In 1975, the *Daily Mirror* newspaper even ran a weekly feature called 'the League of Violence', identifying different clubs' fans' acts of thuggery. This was probably the only league in which Millwall regularly featured near the top.

The Lionesses project was brought in as part of a wider development programme, aimed at trying to reach out to the local community and bring people – other than brainless football thugs – into the life and culture of the club. Jane encouraged me to get involved. But, in truth, I didn't need much persuading.

Millwall held an open training session, and I went along – with 60 or so other girls. It was an eye-opener. Apart from Jane, I'd never played football with other girls before. To me, at the time, it all seemed incredibly professional, and I was in seventh heaven. There were cones and bibs, crash nets, proper training equipment and actual real-life football coaches who really seemed to know what they were doing. This was the business.

I was so full of adrenalin and enjoying myself playing with loads of other like-minded girls for the first time in my life,

I completely lost track of time. It was all just too exciting. But it was an evening session and two bus rides away from where I lived. I came home really late – it was 11 at night – and I got an absolute rocket from my mum. Understandably, she was really worried. I was an 11-year-old girl out by myself in the middle of south London. So, basically, Mum banned me from going there ever again. I was heartbroken, because I'd really impressed at the training session. They'd asked me to play in the Lionesses youth team the following Sunday.

I didn't want to disobey my mum, but this was the opportunity of my young life. There was no way I was going to miss it. So I never told her, and just sneaked out. I played my first game for Millwall, did more than all right, then sneaked quietly back into the house. Each time I had a match or training, I'd make an excuse about going out to see a friend or whatever, and then meet up with my Millwall mates. I didn't like being dishonest and sneaky, but this was my big chance to play proper, competitive football. I really was like the first *Bend It Like Beckham* girl. But it couldn't go on for ever.

As I was becoming more and more involved with Millwall, it became impossible to keep it secret from my mum. So it came to pass that my first big sporting challenge in life was trying to convince her that it was a good thing for me to play football. In my culture, it was not normal for a girl to play. Back in Jamaica, Mum would not have known any girls who played football, it just wasn't done. She had been quite a sportswoman herself at school. But she played 'ladies' sports like netball, hockey and athletics. Football was a manly game.

I pleaded with my mum. Told her how much I loved playing the game and how good I was at it; how well organised and safe things were at Millwall. Why I was so committed to football. I kept chipping away and, over time, Mum began to relent over me playing. A lot of my cousins and friends got pregnant quite young, and Mum began to like the football, because it kept me out of trouble and off the streets. She could also see that it was giving me a real focus in life. Added to that, I was continuing to do well in school, and that was really important to her. So in 1978, aged just 12, she let me officially sign up for Millwall. And then became one of my biggest fans. Mum bought me my first football boots – a pair of Patricks. Up until then, I'd only ever played in trainers.

Carl just thought I was a weirdo. He had the archetypical macho view: football was a man's game and not for little girls. He never came to watch me play, never asked how I was getting on, showed no interest in my football at all. But by this time, I had no interest in him. Except for the hope he'd get out of all of our lives.

It was a very good group at Millwall. We were all the same age and got on well. There was no bullying, no cliques. Was everyone competitive? Absolutely. But there was a lot of camaraderie. So much so that, the following season, they wanted me to go into the first team, to play as an attacking midfielder. I'd scored plenty of goals for the youth side, and was already as skilful as most of the seniors. I said 'no' because all my new friends were in the youth team. The following year, we all went up into the first-team squad together, variously aged just 13 and 14.

At the time, the Lionesses played in the South East Counties League which, like every other club in England, was run by the Women's Football Association. The WFA had formed in 1969, with just 44 member clubs. By 1984 there were 220. At that point in time, there was no such thing as a national league. The women's game was a patchwork of regional leagues up and down the country. It was all pretty amateurish. You'd turn up at 2 p.m. every Sunday, an hour before the match. It was the old oranges on the touchline routine. As the winters progressed, the pitches all turned into complete mud heaps. But the training and coaching was a revelation.

Millwall was where I first met Alan May, who would become one of the biggest influences on my life. He was our coach and very ahead of his time with his ideas. He gave us more ownership of the game and got us thinking more deeply about playing football. Alan would also become a father figure to me. He worked for the old Inner London Education Authority as a coach in the community. As well as Millwall Lionesses he worked in schools, colleges, all over. He treated us as footballers – not women, not men, but footballers. With our team, Alan never did anything different to what he delivered with the boys' sides he coached. What he taught me more than anything – and it's something I've tried to live by throughout my career – is that you can't rely on one person. You're part of a process, that's independent of your own ego. Truly, there is no 'I' in team.

In his day job, Alan worked for BT for 35 years. He was the digital planning manager for London when the capital went from analogue to digital. He was far-sighted in his management style and in implementing management systems. Over the years, he taught me a lot about how he'd operated in industry and how that could help me, first as a footballer and then as a coach. Alan shrewdly realised from early on that I had the potential to coach.

When I later became England manager, one of the first people I turned to was Alan, making him head of my scouting system. He is a gentleman and a gentle man. But he won't take any bullshit, and has been my best and most accurate critic over the years. His attitude has always been, 'I'm not helping you at all, if I just tell you what you want to hear.' So Alan has always been a tough cookie, but I've always known that he's in my corner. If you cut Alan in half, like a stick of rock, he would read 'football' all the way through.

Aged 12, I was still pretty lightweight, so I asked Alan to devise me a fitness schedule that would help me physically develop. I think it quite surprised him that a 12-year-old girl was hassling him for a training programme. To be honest, I was 12 going on 18 when it came to my understanding of the game and my abilities on and off the ball. I'd analysed it forensically ever since I was at primary school. What was missing was physical strength and stamina. I knew I would never be Amazonian, but I needed Alan's help to turn me into a better physical specimen.

From the age of 14, I became ever-present in the Millwall Lionesses, often playing against women two decades my senior. I made my debut in the 1980–81 season against Molesey, with Alan stood watching on the touchline. He thought I was probably the most skilful player on the park that day, but I sure got knocked about a bit. As Alan shrewdly observed at the time, the older players didn't like being given the runaround by a skinny little kid one little bit. It soon toughened me up and, although still small in stature, Alan's fitness schedule made me much more robust. I needed to be. Because back in the early eighties, women's club football in England was rough, tough and very physical. I could beat anyone for pace but some of the players back then were sheer muscle. One of our biggest rivals was Staines, who were horrible. They were real bullies on the pitch. A bit like your Wimbledon of old: nasty and in your face. They were the worst, but plenty of other teams at that time were big, strong and mean. A far cry from the much more skilful women's game of today. I was starting to be talked about in the women's game. Scouts came to see me play. To my amazement, I was called up into the full England squad. I was only 16.

Chapter 2

Three Lions

When I was first selected for the England squad in 1983 there was quite a clique of older players, a lot from Southampton. At the time, they were the best women's side in England. A 20-year-old from Friends of Fulham called Brenda Sempare was also called into the squad for the first time, alongside me. Brenda would later become my partner for a while, but also a lifelong friend. She was an outrageously skilled player, even at 20. For me, she was one of the best players ever to pull on an England shirt.

It didn't take either of us long to realise we were under a lot of scrutiny and the subject of lot of … shall I say, chat … among the older players. Not only were we young, we were also the first two black players to be selected for England. One of the players at the time, Liz Deighan, went to the then England manager Martin Reagan and said Brenda and I were both too small and lightweight. Not strong enough for the rough and tumble of international football. 'You cheeky git,' I thought. She was smaller than me. We might have been two skinny little black girls, but we were physically strong and learnt our football playing on the street with boys. Thanks to Alan May, I was as fit as any of the other players in the England squad.

So Brenda and I were young, shy and didn't feel very welcome. Thank God for Angela Gallimore. A strong, physical Liverpool defender, she'd broken into the squad a year or so before us. Angela had suffered from the cliques and was so fed up with it that she had even considered making herself unavailable for selection for the England squad. She took us under her wing and did everything she could to make us feel at home. I will always be eternally grateful to Angela for supporting me so much in those early days. I still have a treasured present that she bought me. A Brazil shirt, because she reckoned I played as well as a Brazilian. We're still close friends to this day.

I think the situation Brenda and I found ourselves in is common to football in general. New kids arrive on the block and older players feel threatened. I'm not being immodest, but though young, we were both very good players. We had pace and already possessed a lot more technical skill than quite a few of the squad. We were a threat to the old guard and, as a consequence, were not made especially welcome. But shy though I may have been, I was in no way intimidated. I was hungry to play football for my country and refused to let it affect me.

My first cap was against the Republic of Ireland in a European qualifier in September 1983, played at Reading's old Elm Park ground. I came on as a sub with 20 minutes or so to go, as one of the youngest women ever to play for England, aged just 16. We won the game 6–0. I was so excited to go on, but the nervous energy of playing for the first time in an England shirt drained me. I may only have been on for 20 minutes, but when the game finished, I was absolutely knackered. I'd played OK and got a few decent touches on the ball. But it's hard to impose yourself with so few minutes to go.

Martin Reagan, as a player, had turned out on the wing for Hull City, Middlesbrough and Norwich. He was a lovely man, a real old-fashioned gentleman, very softly spoken and gentle in his manner. He had quite a military bearing and it wasn't until many years later that I discovered my old England boss had been a war hero. He'd fought in Normandy during the D-Day landings as a 19-year-old tank commander, and then battled across the Rhine and into Germany. Training with Martin was very old school and army-like. In those days, we'd meet up on a Friday night as a squad and then play on a Sunday. We had very little time together to train or be coached. In the time we had, Martin would always give us the dreaded circuits: six stations, and at each you had to perform a different set of exercises like press-ups, sits-ups, burpees or suchlike. I used to hate it, but that's the way we trained with England in those days.

I can't remember us being given much information about the teams we were about to play, or any analysis of individual players. There wasn't the opportunity or the money for Martin and his tiny number of staff to put anything like that together. There were no scouts to report back on other international sides and the matches they'd played; no TV or even radio coverage of other women's teams, to take notes from.

Martin used to set us up with a lot of purpose. But we were never very sure what to expect from the opposition or how they would look to play. Sometimes ignorance was bliss, and we won games because we had no fear of just going out there and playing. Now and again, we got a battering because we had little idea of how the opposing team would come at us. At the time, it was just the way things were in women's football in this country. You never questioned it and just got on with each game. When I think about

24

how supremely well prepared the England team increasingly became, it is like looking back into an entirely different, almost alien world.

All football has moved on, the men's and the women's game. As a young player, my re-fuelling was burgers and pizzas and, well, a lot of fast food. There'd be good West Indian food from my mum along the way, like our traditional Sunday dinner of rice, peas and chicken. But from the perspective of English football generally, it wasn't until Arsène Wenger took over at Arsenal in 1996 that everyone started to cotton on and think differently about diet. He got experts in to advise his players about nutrition and what different types of diet did to their bodies, and pretty much ushered in a revolution.

Back in the eighties, we hadn't the faintest clue about what we should or shouldn't be eating. Some of the squad were inveterate smokers, and tales about boozy footballers weren't confined to the men's game. That was the culture then, and no one thought twice about it.

One of my enduring memories of Martin is of after a game we won, the staff and most of the players having a good drinking session. I was only 16 or 17 at the time, so didn't drink alcohol. To this day, I hardly ever drink anyway. But everyone got squiffy and started a sing-song. Right at the heart of it was a very merry Martin, who belted out song after song at the top of his voice. I was quite taken aback. But even with a few inside him, he still remained an absolute gentleman. I also remember that Angela got so smashed that Brenda and I had to help her get dressed the following morning, she was so out of it.

We had quite a lot of success, playing under Martin. In May 1984, we made it to the final of the European Competition for

Women's Football, the forerunner of the present UEFA European Championships. Sixteen teams competed in four qualifying groups over a two-year period to reach the two-legged semi-finals and final. We won our group, and then beat Denmark over two legs in the semis. For the final, it was to be Sweden, home and away. We narrowly lost the first leg 1–0 in Gothenburg in a tight, hard-fought match. Pia Sundhage, arguably the world's best player at the time, scored a well-flighted header, and if it hadn't been for some heroics from our goalie Terry Wiseman it could have been more.

Swedish football was so far in advance of our own in terms of its development, it was almost embarrassing. We played in their national stadium, and 60 minutes' worth of match highlights were shown on Swedish TV that evening. After men's football, women's soccer was the second most popular sport in Sweden, and 70,000 regularly played it. In England in 1984, that number was less than 5,000. In Sweden at the time, the government paid women's football a healthy annual grant, and facilities, equipment and sponsors were thrown in for good measure. In neighbouring Denmark, the women's team operated under the umbrella of the men's FA and were generously sponsored by the same brewery as their international male colleagues. In Scandinavia generally, women's football was in a very healthy state.

In comparison, we got minimal press coverage and even battled to find a venue for the second leg. It's hard to believe, we were in a UEFA final and not one single London club, let alone Wembley, God forbid, wanted us to play this showpiece match at their ground. We asked the FA to lean on the clubs, but nothing happened. Some didn't even have the decency to reply to the WFA's requests. Everyone wanted the second leg to be played in the capital to give the women's game some much needed publicity. But London's footballing establishment didn't want to know. The WFA's secretary Linda Whitehead contacted all 13 London football league clubs. They either came right out with it and said they weren't interested in putting on women's football matches, or claimed that their pitches were being dug over in preparation for the new season. It was a real kick in the teeth for the women's game. We'd played out of our skins to get all the way to a prestigious European final and we weren't even offered the incentive of a good ground to play on. It was an embarrassment. The Swedish FA arranged for their women to play the first leg in the country's most prestigious ground, the national Ullevi stadium in Gothenburg. We couldn't even get a fourth division London team to offer us their facilities. I think, for a while, the WFA were genuinely worried that the Swedes might put in a complaint and England could have ended up forfeiting the tie.

At the last minute, Luton Town stepped in and we played the Swedes at Kenilworth Road. Two days of non-stop rain left the pitch looking like a newly ploughed field. It was tipping down with rain, but it didn't deter the Swedish media. A TV crew and 36 reporters and photographers travelled over from Sweden to cover the match.

It was a tough old game of football. The ball kept getting stuck in the mud or pools of water, and the penalty areas were almost unplayable. But we dug in, and our team joker Linda Curl scored in the second half to win the game by a single goal and level the tie at 1–1. Then, in traditional English fashion, we lost 4–3 on penalties. Heartbreakingly, after being our hero in normal time, it was Linda who missed our first penalty, giving the Swedes the psychological edge.

I remember the two teams coming together for a celebration dinner afterwards. Sweden's star striker Pia Sundhage was a talented musician and a bit of a centre-stage kind of girl. There was a grand piano in the restaurant, and she played it and sang along brilliantly. To this day, whenever she is presenting at football events, she always bursts into song, by way of introduction. It's her trademark now.

Just over two thousand hardy souls had turned out to watch the match. Back home in Scandinavia, Sweden's win made front-page news in all the country's newspapers. We managed the odd single paragraph here and there in sports-news round-ups, but that was about it. This was where women's football was at in the 1980s in England: unrecognised and unremarked upon.

That 1984 side was a good one, and things were starting to build. On her day, Pat Chapman could turn the best defences inside out with her ball skills. Her striking partners Linda Curl and Kerry Davis were both quality players. While among the youngest in the squad, Debbie Bampton and Gillian Coultard were beginning to strike up a great understanding together in forward midfield. Goalie Terry Wiseman was probably England's most outstanding player throughout the tournament. But then again, she needed to be.

What we should have had to back up that talent was a future pool of much younger players coming up behind us. But the FA had no youth development structure at all. A Swedish FA official told Martin Reagan that they'd recently held a residential course for 350 selected 11-year-old girls. In a few years' time, we would have to face the products of that hard and intensive work.

In England in 1984 there were few opportunities for girls under 15 to even play football, let alone be coached properly in the game. Many schools actively discouraged girls from playing and despite our success in the UEFA Championships, women's football was still being prevented from moving forward because of a total lack of investment in the grassroots.

After the final, it wasn't quite back to playing in front of two men and a dog. Later in the year I would play in front of nearly 100,000 people in what would be the very first women's football game at Wembley, and it wouldn't be for England. Liverpool and Everton were playing in the Charity Shield, and as a curtain-raiser four women's teams were invited to contest a six-a-side tournament. I had been part of the Millwall Lionesses team that back in July of that year had won the women's national five-a-side football championship in Woking. As a result, we got an invite to play in a six-a-side curtain raiser at the national stadium, alongside St Helens, Merseyside and Wirral, and Howbury Grange from Bexley.

Wembley was a revelation. I'd never played on a pitch like it. It was like gliding across an Axminster carpet; the contrast with the mudbath we'd played on against Sweden at Kenilworth Road couldn't have been greater. We beat Howbury Grange 4–0 to get to the final and I scored a brace. Then we got some surprise news on the touchlines. Originally, the six-a-side final was scheduled to kick off at 1.50 p.m. But now it was to go ahead at 2.25 p.m., when the ground would be packed with close on 100,000 Scousers. The atmosphere was electric.

We played St Helens in the final and the game ended 1–1. Now how about this for bizarre? We were awarded the tournament Cup, because even though it was a draw, our goalie was judged to have picked up the ball fewer times than the St Helens keeper. Penalties and golden goals, yes. But that was one way of deciding a match I'd never come across before or since. So we became the first women's team to ever win a trophy at Wembley.

Bizarrely, although I'd played in a European final just days before, that four-way six-a-side tournament gained more publicity for the women's game than anything previously. I like to think that all four teams showed enough skill to impress the predominantly male audience inside the stadium, few of whom would have seen women playing football before.

And then it was on a plane to Venice. It's fair to say that my appearance caused the WFA secretary Linda Whitehead a headache or two. A couple of days after the Wembley date, I was part of a 16-strong women's squad that was flying out to Italy for a four-nation women's football tournament in Venice. According to the WFA's rules, we weren't supposed to play seven days before an international, but Linda decided to make an exception because of the unusual circumstances. Our squad contained four teenagers: myself at 17, my old friend Jane Bartley, and Raeltine Shrieves, who were also both 17, and Yvette Shrieves, 18. The more experienced Sue Street, Kim Nye and our captain Chris Jackson made up the seven. Only 17, and I was getting to travel all over the world. I was starting to like this 'playing for England' business. The tournament saw us pitted against Italy, West Germany and Belgium. The Italian FA footed the bill for our stay there, which was a good job because at the time the WFA was pretty hard up. We drew 1–1 against both Belgium and Italy, but the Germans were just too powerful and athletic for us, running out 2–0 winners. Eventually we won third place by beating Belgium 2–1 in the play-off.

I knew that I'd impressed the knowledgeable Italian crowds. But I was also sounded out about signing up for two different teams in the semi-professional Serie A women's football league out there. In the end I turned them both down. I was only 17, a Londoner born and bred, and all my friends and family lived in the capital. I know a few English players made it over to the Italian league in the 1980s but, at the time, it wasn't for me.

By the early 1990s, women's football in England underwent a small revolution. The Women's Football Association was disbanded in 1993, and power was transferred to the old enemy of women's football, the Football Association.

The WFA secretary Linda Whitehead, pretty much the organisation's only full-time employee, had worked miracles over the years with extremely limited resources. A big Blackburn Rovers fan, Linda had a genius for sports administration. Later, in 1989, she would be named Sports Administrator of the Year in the *Sunday Times* Sportswoman of the Year awards. At the WFA, working with a team of volunteers, she had to be a jill of all trades, pitching in with whatever needed doing, irrespective of her job description.

To say the WFA was cash-strapped would have been an understatement. Finally, it became inevitable that the FA would step in and wind up the Women's Football Association. One of the first things they did was to make Linda redundant, which caused outrage across the women's game. She was soon back in work though with the South of England Athletic Association, which really was the FA's loss. Henceforward, county FA people dominated the new women's football management committee. For a few years, little progress was made in the development of the game. In the course of time, things would change. Once the FA became persuaded of the importance of women's football, their money and resources became vital to its evolution.

Sometimes things have to get worse before they can get better. And that was certainly becoming true in my life back then. I'd moved out of the Greenwich estate and got my own place. It was great to gain some independence, but I soon realised that, without me and Brian around, life at home for my mum seemed to be getting worse. Carl was becoming ever more the bully, hitting her more and more often.

One night I was staying at a friend's place when Mum rang. The frightened tone of her voice terrified me. I knew that Carl had been bashing her about again. I asked my friend if I could borrow his car. He tried to stop me, but I went so crazy he relented. I drove over to my mum's house and along the way worked out very specifically what I was going to do. I would quietly let myself in and go straight to the kitchen. I would grab the largest chopping knife and stab him in the chest. If I killed him, so be it. I worked through how I would claim self-defence on behalf of my mum for everything he'd done to her. I hated him. But more than anything, I was worried that if I didn't do for him, he'd do for my mum.

As I turned the key in the lock I realised he was there, and my heart began to race. I knew that I was walking into big trouble. A sudden calm came over me. I approached him and squared up. I was terrified, that I do remember. He was a beast of a man. One punch would have knocked me senseless. I tried to appeal to him, to his humane side. As ever, that didn't work. He was still surly, aggressive and abusive. So I said that if he ever touched my mum again, I would simply call the police. I did want to kill him.

A few days later, I spoke with my mum and said this couldn't continue. She had to leave the monster. So we made surreptitious plans to get her out of that nightmare. When the time was right, I hired a van. I enrolled the help of a bunch of friends. I phoned the police and told them we needed their support in moving my mum out of the rotten life she was in. I told them I knew he would be violent, so they absolutely had to be there. I'd found Mum a secret new home and we needed to get her furniture and belongings out of the house, pronto, with as little aggro as possible.

When my friends and I arrived at Mum's house, Carl was utterly threatening, as I knew he would be. He wanted to have a go at everyone, but, thank God, the police did turn up and my friends were bravely supportive. Despite Carl's manic raging and threats, we got Mum out of the house and into a new place where her life could start again. We never saw Carl again.

I deliberated for some time on whether to include this in the book. It's obviously a very personal and sensitive subject. I don't in any way want to hurt or expose my mum. But for women everywhere, it is a story that must be told. There is always a way out, and my mum has gone on to live a happy, fulfilled life, with no fear. She is a wonderful woman who, thank God, got her life back again. If you're a woman in a similar situation, get help, get support and get out.

These experiences go in some way to explaining why I loathe bullies and people who hold unfounded and horrible superiority over others – whether it's because of their gender, their colour or their creed. I experienced many sleepless nights as a child, through fear. I can laugh today, because I'm sure this is why I now love sleep so much.

Chapter 3

Paying to Play

I was in the England team and playing for one of the best women's sides in England. But I was perpetually skint. In the 1980s it cost us all money to play football. First you had to affiliate to the WFA – and then the FA – and pay a fee to whatever league you were in. Then there was the cost of kit, balls, equipment and transport. The biggest cost was probably the hiring of pitches. The more successful a club got the more expensive it became. That meant extra travelling for more competitions, and the costs that went along with that. So we literally had to pay to play.

My subs in the 1980s were £2.50 a week, which might not sound a lot today. But this was 30 years ago, and I came from a background that didn't have money. I well recall Alan, bless him, paying my subs for me – and paying for my soft drinks after matches. He used to have a glasses case in which he kept his change, and I'd be allowed to dip into it for money to buy drinks.

Players were all in the same boat. We ran endless social nights and raffles to pay for equipment and fees. We'd cajole friends, family and even local small businesses and shops into sponsoring our kit. For the 1989–90 season at Millwall, Lionesses supporters Billy Brazil, Pat Watters and Martha Burnige sponsored my tracksuit, boots and kit. Teammate Yvonne Baldeo turned out in full kit courtesy of Duke's Carpets. Maria Luckhurst had her strip sponsored by Clegg Delamare builders – 'no job too small!'

It cost them all the princely sum of £5 towards a tracksuit, £4 for boots, £3 for a shirt, £2 for shorts, and a quid for socks. The Lionesses had a wonderful secretary called Sue Prior, who used to turn her hand to anything to help the club. She even used to take the entire team's kit home to wash it. The kit wasn't custom-made. We were given plain shirts and then had to sew our own badges on. Sue would even help us with that. She was an absolute star.

For so many years, women's football in England only kept running because of the legion of Sue Priors up and down the country, who put in countless unpaid, uncelebrated hours. This book gives me the perfect opportunity to give a huge heartfelt thank you to the uncomplaining and committed army of volunteers who've given so much of their time and energy to the women's game in this country over the years.

Everyone put in the extra miles. As players, we were all queens of the part-time job. Anything we could do to subsidise our football, we did it. In those days, at the highest level, women were footballers for a couple of days a week and then workers for the rest of the week. When I was still at school and playing for Millwall – and then England – I had more Saturday and holiday jobs than you could shake a stick at. I washed dishes, swept floors and worked in factories. My mum worked for the Freemans catalogue company, and she got me work there for a while, processing orders.

In Lewisham precinct, when I was about 15 or 16, I got a job through a friend, as a sales girl in a really high-end men's fashion shop that sold Paco Rabanne suits and designer clothes. I was the only girl working in the shop. Apart from the odd wife or girlfriend that might come in with their partners, I was almost exclusively dealing with men. It gave me the confidence to engage with people who maybe don't perceive you as someone who knows what they're talking about in a male-dominated world.

I learnt a lot about men's suits and how they were cut. I would measure their inside legs, chests and waists, make sure the suits hung well, and advise them on shirts and ties for a good ensemble. A lot of the men who came in didn't expect me, as a young girl, to know anything much about suits. Just in the same way, that throughout my earlier coaching career, a lot of men didn't expect me to know anything about football. So good training there! I quickly learnt to show people I did know what I was talking about and was prepared to speak up for myself.

Working in the shop also taught me a lot about dealing with new people every day, which I often had to do in both my playing and management careers. I learnt how to read people. Whether they were up for a bit of banter or were business-like and just wanted to get on with things; if they were going to be difficult or pernickety. You'd work out tactics and strategies to make sure they'd walk away happy with the transaction and would want to come back. I was a fairly polite teenager anyway, but working with the general public made me realise more and more about the importance of good manners – that if you treated people with respect they were more than likely to do the same to you.

I eventually moved on from men's fashions to sell children's clothes in another shop in the precinct, and then got a Saturday job in a store that sold pretty much everything: collectables, souvenirs, ornaments, kitchenware, you name it. I stayed there for a while as a part-timer and loved the fact that, because of the vast range of things the shop sold, the world and his wife would drop by. At the time, Lewisham was a real cultural melting pot of white Londoners, West Indians, Indians, Pakistanis, Bangladeshis, Turks, Greeks, just about everyone. All ages and races, every class and gender – again, great training for handling the multitude of different people I would meet and work with during my football career. The rest of the staff were good to me and I really enjoyed it there. I worked with a girl called Rose, who had this fantastic voice. At the end of the day, I used to ask her to sing. I've always loved music. I'm a bit of a soul girl and love all the old Tamla and Stax classics. I often wonder what happened to Rose and hope that's she still entertaining people with that incredible voice.

My brother Brian, his future wife Gill and I tried to get temporary jobs together when we were all college students, and for a while we came as a trio. Once, we got work in this local pharmaceutical company. We had to take orders, find them on the shelves, box up the orders and then pack them on to a palette for delivery. We grafted so damned hard that we managed to do two weeks of work in two and a half days, and did ourselves out of the job. I went on to wash dishes again, and my brother got a job in a factory sweeping up tampon casings. A bit later, the three of us got to work together again at Walthamstow Education Authority. I've always had a militant side and, on one of my first days there, one of my bosses said, offhandedly, 'Make me a cup of tea.' I remember looking her up and down and replying, 'Sorry, but I don't believe I was employed to make your tea,' and walked off. I didn't mind grafting at anything. But I wouldn't let people pull rank on me just to show what power they had.

The bottom line was that, during my playing career, I never had any money. Trying to fit in jobs between training and matches was a perpetual balancing act. But soon enough I got a job that actually paid me to coach football and started me off on the road that would take me into management. I worked part-time in sports development through a football in the community project, working in schools and colleges. It was all anti-social hours, a lot of it after school, and the work was sporadic. Often I'd have to sign on to subsidise the work. Sometimes I'd be working with girls, sometimes with boys, now and again with disabled kids. What I learnt early on was that not only did I enjoy coaching, but I had an aptitude for it. I could communicate well and, thanks to Alan May's influence, knew how to drive a coaching session along so that kids stayed interested and engaged.

From my early days at Millwall, I'd watched Alan closely and absorbed what he did to make training enjoyable. It was his belief, and it became mine, that if players found the work boring or repetitive they would only go through the motions, without much commitment. So whenever I coached the kids, I would vary things constantly, try to surprise and excite them. We'd look at formations and individual responsibilities across the pitch. But then also have little contests to see who could do the most keepie-uppies, penalty shoot-outs and individual skills comps.

My start in coaching made me realise even more just how much I loved football and what it can do for people. It teaches kids discipline, teamwork and how to communicate. It helps build self-esteem and self-confidence – often among kids who haven't thus far achieved very much they're happy with in their lives.

The one thing coaching the kids had in common with playing and training as a women's footballer was the bloody awful surfaces we had to work on. We trained on school playing fields and playgrounds around south London: on Clapham Common, but also on Hackney Marshes, anywhere that was cheap or free.

We used to set the goals up ourselves and dismantle them at the end of a session.

I have a theory as to why a lot of the players I grew up with – like Brenda, Debbie Bampton and myself – were so technically skilled. When we were all kids we played street football with the boys, on concrete. When I started at Millwall, a lot of our training sessions took place in schools and colleges after hours. On concrete. When you're playing on hard surfaces, you soon learn to stay on your feet. You learn how to use your centre of gravity and shape your body to ride tackles and avoid being legged over. Because if you are legged over, your knees and elbows get absolutely skinned. That teaches you a lot about poise and balance.

Equally, when you're trying to play on mud-heap pitches you learn through necessity how to precision pass and pick out teammates with much greater accuracy. Otherwise, you're asking them to churn their way through ploughed fields, which over the course of a match is bloody exhausting.

A lot of the games we played were watched by two men and a dog – sometimes it was just the dog. When I look back at the conditions we used to put up with, we really had a lot of dedication and determination. Many of the pitches we played on were disgusting mud-heaps, on which the ball just about rolled. In many ways, we were prepared to play on the worst of surfaces because we just couldn't afford to postpone matches. Travelling up to Liverpool, Doncaster or wherever cost time and money, both of which were in short supply when you played women's football in the 1980s. We'd sweep snow, puddles, anything so as not to cancel a game.

For the longer journeys, we'd hire a small coach. If, say, you were playing in Liverpool, it would be a seven-hour drive up the motorway. You'd arrive, get stripped and go straight out on to the pitch. Then after the game, head straight back into the coach for another seven hours' travel back to south London. You could have flown to New York and back in the same time. Believe me, the buses we used were hardly air-conditioned luxury coaches either. They were generally real boneshakers, so there was little chance of getting any sleep during the journeys.

Once, to save money on an away trip to play the Doncaster Belles, we hired a minibus. There were just enough seats for everyone, but no room for all the kit. We all had to sit on it for the 300-mile round trip. You'd often get back home late at night on a Sunday after an away game, and then most of the girls would have to be up early the next day for work.

Sometimes we'd have to travel up the night before a match if it was an early kick-off. Wherever possible we'd try to get the cheapest accommodation available to save on the pennies, which meant staying in a lot of extremely basic, small hotels and guesthouses. The worst was a place in Doncaster that advertised itself as a hotel but was, as we discovered, some rooms above a scabby nightclub. It was a freezing Saturday night in the middle of winter and, as we arrived in the town, we were amazed to see groups of young girls wandering along the streets, coming in and out of pubs and clubs dressed in nothing but tiny skirts, skimpy tops and high heels. No coats or jackets. 'Bloody hell,' I thought, 'this is what they mean by tough northerners.' We were given keys to our rooms. It was like the Land that Public Health Forgot. If you stood for too long in the same place, your feet stuck to the carpets, they were so wet and manky. The rooms were so cold that night, most of the girls slept in their coats and hoodies. Not that anyone slept much, because booming disco music was coming up through the floorboards until after 2 a.m. The following morning, I remember going into the bathroom for a quick bath, and immediately deciding against it. There was mildew all over the shower curtain, and the bath was filthy. Generally, I'd like to bet players in the Blue Square league got better accommodation than we used to.

In those days prior to the influence of Arsène Wenger, our re-fuelling on trips away consisted of Hobson's choice: a motorway service station or another motorway service station. So it was burger and chips, sausage and chips, anything greasy with chips. The choice was: eat it or don't. Back in the eighties and nineties, motorway service stations in this country were truly bloody awful.

Despite the crap conditions, I'd been really happy at Millwall for nine great years. Kids like Raeltine Shrieves, Jane Bartley and myself had grown up through the ranks together. We used to travel on the bus with our bags, to our home games at Millwall's training ground at Ravensbourne in Bromley. Then we'd have a few drinks together afterwards. The girls at Millwall had become my social life, and many of them had become close friends. Friends or not, I always wanted to win. Even in my late teens, I was beginning to let my teammates know what I thought about our play out on the pitch. The girls still laugh about my first 'team talk'. We were playing Aylesbury and getting hammered – 2–0 down at half-time, but it should have been a lot more. Though I was only 17 or so, I stormed into our dressing room and laid into the rest of the players. Did we want to get stuffed? Were we happy with ourselves? If not, what were we going to do about it? Everyone just sat back in shock. But then we got talking. About how we could change things in the second half.

Alan stood back and let me get on with it. That day he saw something in me. Could I be a manager? My 'team talk' was hardly Churchillian. It was barely coherent, really, but it did get everyone fired up. We went on to win 4–2.

We were a successful team, too – but always the bridesmaids to the Friends of Fulham team. They were invariably champions of the new Greater London League, and we'd be runners-up or thereabouts. Tottenham and Aylesbury were good clubs. But it was always Friends of Fulham who were one step ahead of us all. So in 1987, after so many good years at Millwall, I decided to make a change and move to Friends of Fulham. I must confess that my decision was heavily influenced by the fact that my then partner Brenda Sempare was playing for them. It gave us the opportunity to be together more. And Fulham were a pretty good team. As well as Brenda, the side included fellow England internationals Terry Wiseman, Marieanne Spacey and Terry Springett, plus Ireland international Cathy Hynes. Just two years previously, they'd won the Women's FA Cup final.

Oddly, playing for Fulham was the only time in women's football when I was slagged off for being black. In my experience, racism was fairly rare in the women's game back then. That's what made it so surprising. During a game, one of the opposition called me a black something-not-very-nice, which triggered a sequence of events that was like something out of a comedy show. Teammate Brenda completely lost the plot and went for this girl. She started fighting her and soon they went down in a heap on the ground and rolled around on the pitch, belting lumps out of one another. My brother Brian was watching from the touchlines, a long way away in the distance. You have to bear in mind that Brian wears glasses and doesn't have the greatest eyesight in the world. Suddenly, he came striding across the pitch and raced over towards them, looking like he was going to get stuck in too. Then he spotted me a few yards away and stopped in his tracks. He looked down at the scrapping couple and shrugged, 'Oh, it's you, Brenda.' And with that he galloped back off to the touchline. From a distance, Brenda and I did look very similar. Both slight in build and with our hair swept back. But once Brian had realised his mistake, he left her to it. Brenda and the girl who'd abused me were pulled apart. But that wasn't the end of it. At the end of the game, Brenda followed this girl into the changing rooms and started beating the crap out of her. We all had to pull them apart, but not before Brenda had bashed lumps out of the girl.

I had a really enjoyable two-year spell at Friends of Fulham, which included an appearance at the 1989 Women's FA Cup final against Merseyside team Leasowe Pacific. The week before, tragedy had struck Liverpool in the shape of the Hillsborough disaster, and everyone observed a minute's silence. I scored twice but we were beaten 3–2. The match was played at Old Trafford, which was a big thrill. Not a great audience, though. The final attracted just 914 spectators. But it was broadcast on Channel 4 as a one-hour highlights package the following day, which was progress.

Brenda and I split up and it became awkward being on the same team and training together. Plus, I was missing my old teammates, Alan and the Millwall set-up generally. I returned to a very good Millwall side. In goal, Lesley Shipp was an England international, while young defender Maria Luckhurst was turning out for the England under-21 side. Sue Law, Tina Mapes and Lou Waller were all England internationals. Sue would go on to manage and become chair of the Lionesses. Debbie Bampton played with me in midfield. She was in the middle of a 19-year England career and at the very peak of her game. Kiwi international

Maureen Jacobson was the engine of the midfield. Raeltine Shrieves made her way into the first-team squad from being reserves captain. She would later switch sports and represent Ireland's rugby team. Her sister Yvette played for us too. She would go on to spend two years as a pro in the Italian League playing for Juve Siderno. Our winger, Yvonne Baldeo, had just rejoined Millwall after a season in Serie A with ACF Milan. My old friend Jane Bartley was a regular in the Welsh national side and had turned out for Millwall over 300 times. Myself, I entered that season averaging 1.25 goals per game in women's football, playing from midfield.

I had a truly memorable time back with Millwall. In 1991, we won the Greater London League, seeing off the likes of rivals Arsenal and Friends of Fulham. This qualified us to play the following season in the first ever women's national league, the FA Women's Premier League in 1991–92. But perhaps an even more pleasing triumph came that season when we beat the mighty Doncaster Belles 1–0 at Tranmere's Prenton Park, to win the Women's FA Cup for the first time.

To put it in context, the Belles were just about the best team around at the time. They were the reigning Cup holders, and in the previous eight seasons had featured in the final seven times, winning four. They had an astonishing record in their northern regional league. Up to 1991, they had been unbeaten for four seasons. Their team contained the England captain, Gillian Coultard, and a clutch of other top internationals. The match itself was a titanic struggle, a real war of attrition . But our winger Yvonne Baldeo settled the game in the 65th minute with the only goal of the match. After losing out twice, at last I had my hands on a Women's FA Cup final winner's medal.

But life moves on. The team broke up in the aftermath of that success. A number of the Millwall players had a fallout with the chairman and went off to play for Arsenal. Generally, the vibe at Millwall had turned a bit sour. So Sue Law, Alan May and myself decided to try something new – to create a totally new club. And so Bromley Borough was born.

It was an exciting time for all of us, but the work and energy required to set up something new was exhausting. We had to recruit a full squad of players, sort out a stadium to play in, and arrange training facilities. Then there was the funding, and all the admin that's required in setting up something fresh. And we were dealt an initial disappointment that gave us a little mountain to climb.

Though we'd quickly enrolled a good number of top players and internationals, the FA played a straight bat against the idea of us being fast-tracked up a few leagues. Given the ability of the squad, it would have been nonsense to start us off on the very bottom rung. The FA decided to start us off on the very bottom rung. So in 1991, Bromley Borough started their first season in the Eastern Counties League, which was ludicrous. Virtually every game we played was a complete mismatch. We frequently scored well into double fingers against our opponents. We tried to be gracious about it, but it was often really embarrassing. Bromley fielded players every week that were in a totally different class from the women we were playing against. In the men's game, it would be a bit like putting Chelsea or Arsenal into the Conference. Unsurprisingly, Bromley Borough remained unbeaten for three seasons, achieving three successive promotions as champions and giving a lot of sides a complete pasting. In 1993–94, we won the National League Division One South by ten points. That secured us promotion into the then top flight of English women's football, the FAW Premier League.

But it was time for more change. To become an even stronger outfit, we all sat down and considered an offer that had been put to Bromley. During the close season of 1994–95, we entered into a merger with Croydon FC and enlisted Debbie Bampton as manager. We played our first season in the Premier League as Croydon Women's FC and ended the year in fourth place. It was a strong team. I would become one of six players from Croydon who would represent England at the World Cup.

Chapter 4

From the Old Kent Road to Sweden

1994 proved to be a very special year for me, personally. One summer evening I went for a night out with friends at the Frog and Nightgown nightclub on the Old Kent Road. I got chatting with a woman called Michelle, who worked in corporate hospitality for American Airlines, and we talked about our experiences of working in America. She'd just spent a year in the States, and I wasn't long returned from a few months working as a youth coach on a soccer camp in Minneapolis. We hit it off, started seeing one another, and over 20 years later are still together.

To begin with, Michelle had absolutely no interest in football. She had no idea that I was an England player, or that there were such things as women's football leagues. She was a tennis nut and soon got me into that, too. But, over time, Michelle saw how much football meant to me and so started to explore it more. The first live game I took her to was Arsenal v Aston Villa at Highbury, in the old Coca-Cola Cup. I wouldn't say she became an overnight convert but she really enjoyed the spectacle. From there, I took Michelle to some women's games and she began to see that it wasn't just a kickabout for us – that we had a lot of skill and, more than anything, total commitment. To begin with, she started to come to my matches just because we were partners. After a while, she started getting into it for herself. Now Michelle is a big fan.

I've always been really well supported by family and friends. After her early days of not wanting me to play football – it wasn't what West Indian girls did – my mum became my number one fan. She loved coming to watch me play. She'd often travel on the supporters' bus for various club and international games. My brother Brian and my sister-in-law Gill would come too, and it used to give me that extra little something out there on the pitch, when I knew that they were in the crowd. Throughout 1994–95, Michelle and my family and friends had a lot of good football to watch, as England swept their way through qualifying for the 1995 UEFA European Championships.

The big carrot for doing well in the 1995 UEFA European Championships was qualification for the second ever FIFA Women's World Cup, later that year in Sweden. The top five European teams were guaranteed to go. So we were all keen to find out from UEFA who we'd be up against in the Euro qualifying group. There were only six qualifying games, but they were drawn out over two years because so many of the international teams were totally amateur, and players had full-time jobs to do between the training and the matches.

We came out of the pot in Group 7, alongside Spain and Belgium, and little Slovenia. Spain were the real threat, but we managed to play out two 0–0 draws against them, home and away. The key games for us were against Belgium. Best them, and we were realistically at least runners-up in the group. We travelled to Koksijde on Belgium's North Sea coast and pulled off a 3–0 away win. We played the return in Nottingham and ran out 6–0 winners.

If we hadn't beaten Slovenia twice – and by a lot of goals – we really didn't deserve to pull on an England shirt. Slovenia were at a very early stage of their development and, though not a pub side, were akin to the club teams I'd played for a decade previously. Part of the break-up of the old Yugoslavia, Slovenia had only had its first democratic election in 1990 and was still trying to build its economy. Their FA had very little money – everything was funded on a shoestring. These European qualifying games were their first matches in international football. What a baptism of fire. We flew to their capital Ljubljana first, played them on a building site of a pitch, and won 10–0. Our home fixture against them was at Brentford's Griffin Park, and once again we cruised it 10–0. I came on as sub and scored with my first touch.

As Belgium managed a win against the Spanish, our 0–0 draw at home to Spain meant we were group winners and through to the knockout stage. England had scored 29 times in their six games and didn't concede a single goal.

Each of the qualifying group tables told the story of the uneven development of women's football across Europe at that time. In our group, Slovenia conceded 60 goals in their six games and didn't manage to score once. Spain put 17 past them in Palamós. They wouldn't play another competitive match for over a decade.

In other groups, Wales conceded an average of six goals a game; the Czechs let in 23 goals in their six games. Most of the groups were won by runaway winners who scored hatfuls of goals. The gap between the best, the worst and, indeed, many of the sides in between, was massive. I remember feeling that if women's football was ever going to progress as a sport and be taken seriously by the wider world, that gap in ability had to be narrowed. I didn't realise back then, though, that one day trying to achieve that would become my all-consuming passion in work for UEFA and FIFA. For the less developed teams to improve, they had to get competition against the better sides.

The four group winners played out two-legged home and away semi-finals. We were drawn against Germany and, in December 1994, got hammered 4–1 at home to put the tie beyond our grasp. The following February we played the return leg in front of 7,000 fans in Bochum and put in a far better performance, losing 2–1.

But getting that far meant we were through to the second ever FIFA Women's World Cup in Sweden, alongside China, Japan, Nigeria, Brazil, USA, Canada, Australia, Denmark, Germany, Norway and the hosts. It was a bizarre arrangement, really. The European countries had decided to use the European Championships as the qualification for the World Cup – which would take place just four months after the Euros. Whatever, we were there.

It was the biggest thrill of my young life to go to a World Cup. But the actual world of international women's football in the mid-nineties was very different from today. The attention around it didn't feel as good as it does now. The way we prepared, the mode of transport, it was all so different. We went from one part of Sweden to another on night trains. We didn't get an ounce of sleep, thanks to the noise from other passengers, the juddering motion of the trains and the roar of the engines. We slept in tiny bunks beds in little sleeper cabins and, for me, sleep was virtually impossible. The five tournament venues were all in cities a long way apart. So with a game every other day, we were on Swedish trains a lot.

It just wouldn't happen now, as we're so conscious of the importance of the players getting refreshed with a good night's rest. But everything was done on an absolute shoestring. Even though we were at the World Cup, we were playing in men's kit. For players of my size, the shirts and shorts were so baggy, and two or three times too big.

There was no thought about diet and nutrition, and we ate what we were given in the hotels. If I remember rightly, herring often featured, which I guess is pretty healthy. But every other day?

This was also long before the days of central contracts, and my teammates all worked in a wide range of different jobs. Gill Coultard was a factory worker, Donna Smith was a firefighter, and Clare Taylor a postwoman. Deb Bampton was working as a chauffeur in central London. Some of the girls in the squad had to take unpaid leave from work just to be there. Marieanne Spacey had her workmates to thank for being in Sweden. Her boss refused her time off from her job as a fitness instructor in a leisure centre. She had to beg sympathetic workmates to cover her shifts.

I was still working as a coach in the community, and at a couple of football clubs with their youngsters. So I was able to be a bit more flexible. Even so, I was paid by the hour, so when I wasn't working I wasn't earning. At the time, England players were basically just paid pocket money when they were away for matches and tournaments. It's probably hard for younger women players today to understand, but my trip to a World Cup left me completely out of pocket. Although playing for my country was an incredible honour, it also felt a little like doing voluntary work.

Apart from the players, the entire back-up team numbered just five people: our manager, Ted Copeland; his assistant; a doctor; a physio; and an administrator. Just by way of comparison, Mark Sampson's 2015 World Cup squad was looked after by a back-room team of 25 people.

Ted had been England manager since 1993 and brought an unusual footballing background to the table. Though he'd had a spell as first-team coach at Hartlepool United, he'd spent over a decade working as a lecturer in physical education at a university in Saudi Arabia, where he also coached the Saudi under-16 and under-19 national teams. In 1990, Ted took on the role of the FA's regional director of coaching for the north of England. Then, three years later, added the part-time role of England women's coach to his duties.

I learnt a lot from Ted. I'd already started to get my coaching badges, and had begun to look more closely at how managers and coaches went about their work. I think it was the first time, under Ted, that I was introduced to a proper A licence perspective. He brought a lot of new coaching ideas to the England squad, which was really refreshing. I was fascinated by how he structured the content and the delivery of his training and coaching sessions. He was meticulous in his preparation.

I'd always been a natural ball player and a midfielder. But for this, our first ever World Cup tournament, the manager took me along as a squad defender. At the time we struggled defensively, and I could play anywhere. Ted also wanted a bit of pace at the back which, before later injuries, I had in abundance. So I was given the number 2 shirt, but to be quite honest, I was just grateful to be there.

For the whole squad, it was not to be a time for expansive football. Ted didn't really like ball players, he was more of a long-ball devotee. His ambition was to keep us in the tournament for as long as he could. For that he believed we needed to get the ball into the final third good and quick. In truth, we weren't within touching distance of the best sides at the time, and Ted was probably right. But it was frustrating to play in that style.

Not that I played much. Ted had me on the bench for the opening group match against Canada, and for subsequent games. We beat the Canadians 3–2 in Helsingborg. I came on as sub towards the end of the second half and, almost immediately, put in a cross from the right for Gill Coultard to score with her head. That put us 3–0 up, and despite Canada coming back at us with two last-gasp goals, it proved to be the winner. Three–two, and we had three points on the board.

Then it was back on the night train. This time to Karlstad, which was over 400 kilometres north of Helsingborg. I was always keen on geography at school and, at one point, had memorised all the capital cities of the world. But I had no idea just how big Sweden was. The matches came thick and fast, so there was little time for rest or recuperation. The second game was against one of the tournament favourites, Norway. They were a big, strong team and, in truth, we did well to keep the score down to 2–0. I came on as sub again, and it was great to play in front of what was then a big crowd for women's football – 5,500. The Scandinavian attitude to women's football in the 1990s was a million miles more enlightened than the way we were viewed back in England.

Next up was Nigeria, who had lost their first group game 8–0 to Norway, but had improved to hold Canada 3–3 in their second. They were looking for a win to qualify, as indeed were we. For us, Nigeria were an unknown quantity. Though Ted Copeland had done what homework he could, we weren't quite sure just what to expect. Again, I was named on the bench. On the pitch, it was another good performance from the girls. We were 3–1 up inside 40 minutes, and though Nigeria got a late goal, we stayed in control to win 3–2. We were out of the group stages and into the quarter-finals of the World Cup.

In the last eight we faced Germany, already one of the best international teams in the world. It meant another train, this time to Västerås, west of Stockholm. Again, there was little time to acclimatise to our new surroundings or even get some time out on the training pitch. We played the Germans in front of 2,317 fans at the Arosvallen Stadion. From the off, Germany were better, quicker and stronger than us, in virtually every department. If it hadn't been for a superb performance from our goalie, Pauline Cope, and some backs-to-the-wall defending from the rest of us, we could have got a hammering. We held out for most of the first half, spending a lot of time in our own final third. But just before half-time, the Germans scored their inevitable opening goal. Anoushka Bernhard played a slide-rule pass into the feet of Martina Voss, who stroked it home from just inside the box.

After the break, they came forward in waves and soon their greater fitness and athleticism began to wear us down. We were knackered and, despite players putting their bodies on the line in a long series of last-ditch tackles, Germany scored two more through Maren Meinert and Heidi Mohr. Germany ran out 3–0 winners, and ultimately went on to become tournament runners-up, losing out in the final to Norway, 2–0. England were going home.

It was a strange experience. It was wonderful to be at a World Cup, no matter how under-developed the tournament. But I spent so little time on the pitch – brought on twice late in the second half in two games, and an unused substitute in the third. In later years as manager, I know that some players who had bit parts in tournaments didn't think I understood how they were feeling. Been there, done it. Later in my England career I found myself on the bench more often, and it's tough. Every player wants to play. But a manager can only have 11 on the pitch at any one time.

The 1995 World Cup had been an important step forward for women's football in Europe. The competition gained a lot of media coverage across mainland Europe, though, as ever, precious little in England. Women's football had pulled in its first major global sponsor in confectioners, Mars, and people were slowly becoming more aware of the game. Even Diana Ross!

On our way back home, the squad were all in the departure lounge at Stockholm Airport for our flight back to England. Who should be waiting there too, but Ms Ross and her 'people'. It seemed bizarre to see her in Sweden. I was a big Diana Ross fan, but wasn't a celebrity autograph hunter. I was happy to sit back and just watch Diana with her entourage and say I'd been there.

That wasn't the case for some of my teammates, who were desperate to talk to her and to get the great diva to sign something for them. So a little group of England players trooped respectfully over to Diana Ross and her crew. The look on her face was priceless – who are these creatures? Get them away from me. She wasn't remotely interested in making any kind of contact with my teammates, and got her security people to get rid of them. It was quite depressing diva behaviour and, to be honest, I rather went off Diana Ross after that. I wouldn't for a second put myself in a league anywhere near the fame of Ms Ross. But I would discover later, when I became England manager, that when you're in the public eye, life becomes a goldfish bowl.

Chapter 5

Croydon

So it was back to domestic football. Everything at Croydon was falling into place. I'd been made captain in the close season. England stalwart Debbie Bampton was now player-manager. Brenda had moved over from Friends of Fulham to join us. The side was full of real characters and top players like Kerry Davis, Sammy Britton and Joanne Broadhurst – 1995–96 would be my best ever in domestic football.

In the close season, Michelle had been voted in as Croydon's chairperson. She'd grown more and more enthusiastic about women's football, and wanted to use her experience from working in the corporate world to help fundraise for the club. Michelle was particularly concerned that the players had to dip so deeply into their own pockets, just to play. So she set about trying to get sponsors. Her old employers, American Airlines, chipped in with some airline tickets. They were raffled off to raise cash. She managed to get some money out of the local *Croydon Advertiser*, and saved a lot of cash by getting everyone from local printers and sports outfitters to pledge us some free stuff.

As footballers, we were all, of course, used to chipping in to pay for transport and overnight accommodation. But Michelle was appalled that we were playing for one of English football's top women's teams, and yet always out of pocket. Her fundraising certainly helped matters for a while. But life in the women's leagues in the in the 1990s was still a hand-to-mouth existence.

Halfway through the season, we were playing well and winning games. Michelle felt moved to make a prediction that a lot of people later put down to the enthusiasm of the new chair. She said we would win the league and Cup Double. What a lot of people learnt at Croydon was: don't bet against Michelle.

We got to the Women's FA Cup final and played Liverpool at Millwall's Den. I'd been having hamstring problems, and my right leg was heavily strapped and bandaged. But there was no way I was missing the final. Before the match, Alan put me through a fitness test. It was tougher than I had trained all year. Or at least that's what it felt like. But there was no reaction from the hamstring, and I was in the final. Just over two thousand fans turned up at the Den. Karen Burke scored the opener for them on 22 minutes. But I put us back in it with a shot from inside the box just before half-time. The rest of the game got bogged down in midfield, though we did have our chances. Eventually, the final went to penalties. I scored mine and Croydon ran out 3–2 winners on pens. I had my hands on a Women's FA Cup winner's medal for the second time.

The game was also significant in that Liverpool's Rachel Brown became the youngest player ever to play in a WFA final, aged just 15. What was so impressive about this was the position in which she played. It's a big enough ask playing at the top at such a tender age in an outfield position. But to be mature enough to take on the responsibility of goalkeeper, shows why Rachel was always destined to go all the way in the game. Under my management, she would later become an England regular. She was a valuable, optimistic squad member to have around off the pitch, too.

After winning the FA Cup, we then found ourselves with a ludicrous fixture pile-up in the Premier League. Thanks to our Cup run and a bad winter of match cancellations, we had to play five games in ten days. We were lying in second place behind the Doncaster Belles. We had five games in hand. But they had a 13-point lead over us.

It was an exciting end to the season, but total mayhem. Rare for the women's leagues, we had to play games in midweek, some away from home. Players were having problems getting time off work and organising childcare. I was desperate to play in every game and, in retrospect, probably pushed myself too hard. My hamstring needed constant treatment and attention. But we all held our nerve. Croydon won four and drew one out of our five games in hand. We pipped the Belles on goal difference to become champions. Croydon were Double winners and had well and truly arrived. But I ended the season totally crocked. And not from my hamstring problems.

Our last game had been against rivals Arsenal. Along with Brenda, I was one of our flair players, someone who made things happen. Arsenal decided to give us both a real good roughing up. Halfway through the match, I was through on goal. An Arsenal defender went straight through me. I remember flying up into the air and landing in a painful heap. I was in agony but didn't realise at the time what I'd done to myself. I got subbed but stayed on at the ground until the final whistle. Then it was off to A & E, where I discovered I had a dislocated collarbone – so quite an end to our Double-winning season.

For the next couple of years, I enjoyed one of my happiest spells in domestic football. The atmosphere at Croydon was special. Everyone pitched in: partners, parents and families of the players all helped out; as volunteers in the clubhouse, helping to roll and tend to the pitch, ferrying players here and there. Apart from the guy who was steward of the clubhouse, I don't think anyone got paid. It was all volunteer work. But always done with such good grace and enthusiasm.

Then, of course, there was Mother Theresa. She was the mum of one of our players, Columbine Saunders, and just happened to be called, well, Theresa. Most women's football clubs at that time had a Mother Theresa. At Millwall we'd had Sue Prior who turned her hand to everything. At Croydon, we had Mother Theresa. She was the treasurer, the kit person, she'd make the tea, help roll the pitch. All totally unpaid, of course.

We shared our stadium, the Croydon Arena on Albert Road, with a men's football team and the Croydon Harriers athletics club, whose members included the Olympic shot-putter Judy Oakes. The ground had been revamped in the early nineties and it had a grandstand that held a couple of hundred fans. There was an athletics track between the terracing and the pitch, which put some distance between the fans and the players. During close-season training, when Debbie was trying to get everyone fit after the summer break, I well remember running round and round that bloody track. I like running, but not in circles.

With two senior men's and women's teams playing regular fixtures at the ground, no matter how much work was done to keep the pitch in good repair, it was always in pretty poor condition. Particularly in the depths of winter.

After matches, everyone used to get together for a drink in the clubhouse. The fans and players all pretty much knew one another by name. The place would be piled high with sandwiches, snacks and cakes and there'd always be a raffle to help raise more funds. It would be really amusing to watch Mother Theresa zipping around the clubhouse trying to get players to cough up their subs – the girls all walking off swiftly in the opposite direction. Depending on how many hours I'd worked that week, that sometimes included me.

For the first three years of Croydon's time in the FAW Premier League we did a lot of travelling. Our only local opponents were Arsenal, Wembley and Millwall. So we spent a lot of time on the motorway travelling to places like Doncaster, Wolverhampton, Ilkeston, Southampton and, particularly, to Liverpool – back then Liverpool, Everton and Tranmere Rovers all featured in the Premier League. It was hard work for everyone fitting football in alongside jobs, being mums or doing college study. But six or seven years in, the truly national Women's Premier League had started to give women's football more of a profile and a following. Websites and fanzines were springing up, and slowly more people were getting the message that women's football was on the move. Little did I realise it, but so was I.

I always had an issue with my hips and my calves, and with cramp. Even when I was a young player, I took salt tablets for the cramps. But that did me no good. I saw plenty of doctors about it. One advised me to stop playing. I told her she was incompetent. Now, my injuries were catching up on me, and I was increasingly thinking more about coaching. I knew the end of my playing career couldn't be too many years away, and I needed to start thinking about the future. Whoever came up with the cliché 'whatever doesn't kill you makes you stronger' didn't work in sport. As all footballers know, the more you're injured, the more you get injured. Old wounds never fully heal, they leave players with lasting areas of physical vulnerability and weakness. I think for most footballers, injuries are the biggest fear. You try to endure and manage a long catalogue of niggles and more serious setbacks throughout your playing days. But you're ever mindful you may just be one tackle, challenge or accident away from that final injury – the one that brings the curtain down on your career.

I look now at what the players have on the medical side, in terms of support and care. I wish I could have had a fraction of that when I was playing. A physio and a doctor would turn up for international get-togethers, and that was about it. In between the games, there was no help. The women's clubs were all run on a shoestring, so they had little to offer. If you were injured or had a problem, you were pretty much on your own. It was A & E, or you had to pay for your own treatment, which I did often throughout my playing career.

When I played, I was all-action. So not surprisingly I picked up my fair share of injuries along the way. I regularly pulled muscles in my hamstrings. Once, I dislocated my shoulder. After I retired, I discovered that the constant wear and tear on the muscles around my hip had worn them down and I had no muscle protection on the joint. Recent research by FIFA suggests that women are between two and six times more likely to suffer from this, because of generally having wider hips, which increase the leg's angle into the knee. And that no matter how much you condition, women do have weaker hamstrings. I'm sure women footballers of my generation also suffered more injuries because of the conditions of the pitches and training areas we played on. It was either mud or concrete, with very little of any quality in between.

The worst injury I suffered by far during my playing career was during my two-year spell at Friends of Fulham. I snapped an Achilles tendon, which kept me out of the game for one long year. It was the season after our WFA final runners-up match against Leasowe Pacific, and, once again, we'd progressed to the Cup semi-final. We were training at Ferndale School in Brixton on a hard, concrete surface. I turned with the ball and my Achilles snapped like a rubber band. It was ruptured. I tried to get up and run around again, but totally collapsed. I had surgery pretty much straight away. Because the semi-final was coming up, I tried to get myself discharged so I could get to the match. But they wouldn't let me leave. I was so upset, because I wanted to be a part of it all, even if I wasn't playing.

I was put on a ward for the elderly – people who needed to get out of bed to improve their mobility. This male nurse treated me like I was elderly too, not a fit, healthy international sportswoman. He ordered me out of bed and told me to start moving around. That was the last thing I wanted to do with such an injury, and I told him so in no uncertain terms. I knew how much it would hurt, and not help my recovery. I'd wanted to go to the toilet, but refused to use a bedpan because I just felt so embarrassed, more than anything. I swung myself out of the bed and the pain in my leg was unbelievable. The weight of the cast on the wound caused me mind-numbing hurt, but I wasn't about to show it.

Everything went wrong. Six weeks later they took the cast off and discovered my foot was at the wrong angle. So it had to be re-plastered. Then, while I was on crutches, I slipped on a wet patch, put my foot down too hard and the stitches split. I passed out with the pain. So it was back to hospital to get it re-stitched.

There was no help from the FA with injuries, so basically you had to pay for rehab yourself. I was so lucky to find a really good physio who did it for a minimal fee. Otherwise, I don't know how I would have afforded it. Once I was off the crutches, one of the first things she did was teach me how to walk again. Your walking pattern and gait changes. So there was plenty of stretching and walking in front of a full-length mirror, to get the new walking pattern right.

I tried to stay involved with my teammates, and I'd go to all the matches. But it was really hard not playing. Over the next few months, I slowly progressed from walking to jogging to running. Getting back into training, after so long out, completely exhausted me. I soon realised that I had also lost a good yard of pace. And that's not great when a lot of your game is based on sheer speed.

These injury experiences all made me acutely aware that there should be more help and support available for, at the very least, the top players in the women's game. As my 1997–98 season with Croydon was drawing to a close, I had no idea how near I might be to help alter that culture. Almost overnight, my life was about to change for ever.

Chapter 6

Sweet FA

It was early June 1998 and World Cup fever was seizing the country. England were off to France, and every other car in the middle of London seemed to have a little St George's flag waving from its side. As David Beckham and the boys took the short trip over the Channel to ultimately crash out in the last 16 to Argentina, my football season – my eighth for Croydon – was drawing to a close. Little did I realise at the time, but my entire playing career was about to come to a complete end in the most unexpected of ways.

We were having another good season at Croydon. But even though still comparatively young as a footballer, my hips and hamstrings were really beginning to feel a lot of wear and tear. I'd done my coaching badges up to the B licence and was having more and more thoughts about building towards a career in coaching when I got a call from the FA asking me into their Lancaster Gate headquarters 'for a chat'. I was hoping it might be about becoming involved with some youth-team coaching, but wasn't feeling overly confident. A few months earlier I had applied for a job with the FA as a regional development officer, but didn't get it. To be honest, I hadn't been too bothered. But I really did want to try to get my foot in the door at the FA. I put on my one and only vaguely business-like suit and headed into central London.

I'd never been to 12 Lancaster Gate before, and it was incredibly plush. I'm a very visual person, and I was drinking it all in. Right next to the beautiful greenery of Hyde Park, in the most exclusive terrace of buildings, the place must have been worth a fortune. It was very old school, a labyrinth of stairs, doors and corridors over five floors, with lots of highly polished wood. I was kept waiting for ages. But people were really pleasant and brought me endless cups of tea. In hindsight, I realised my 'chat' was running so late because something bad had hit the fan, as I would later learn it always seemed to do at the FA.

Whoever was going to interview me was probably out fire-fighting somewhere. The 'whoever' turned out to be Robin Russell, a man who worked closely with Howard Wilkinson, who was then the FA's technical director. A former manager at Leeds United and Sheffield Wednesday, Howard was in charge of coaching and other training programmes at all levels of the game. Sitting next to Robin was Kelly Simmons, head of women's football at the FA. Apart from secretaries, PAs and cleaners, she was one of the few women working at Lancaster Gate, and virtually the only one with a post at any management level in the building. I was given yet another cup of tea and, after some small talk between the three of us, Robin smiled and said, 'Hope, I'd like to offer you the England job.' Inside me a thousand jaws dropped. It hadn't crossed my mind for a second that this is what the interview would be about. The 'chat' was about me becoming manager of the England Women's team. *What?!*

My heart began to race, I was so shocked. Inside, I was thinking, 'What the hell have you just said?' It didn't register. But

I kept my poker face on. I betrayed not one single bit of emotion. I simply said, 'I'll think about it.' Robin stared at me with a look that said, 'Is this woman the full bloody ticket?' He was Howard Wilkinson's co-pilot, sent to suss out and deliver the new England manager. And she wasn't playing ball.

Don't get me wrong. Inside, I was massively excited. But they were asking me to make what was a potentially life-changing decision. I had a lot to think about, and I wished that at this point, they'd just asked me to go home and mull it over.

But then Robin did something that really shocked me. He took me along a corridor to show me around the then England manager Glenn Hoddle's office. It was meant to impress me. And all I could think was, 'Why are you doing this? If you knew me, you just wouldn't have done this.' I just played it cool. I tried to look totally unimpressed with the whole thing. Which, frankly, I was. I listened to what else they had to say and told them again that I'd think about it. They gave me seven days to make up my mind.

I got back home to south London, but Michelle was out. So I went around to see Brenda. Though we were no longer partners, we'd become great friends, and I trusted her no end. I wanted her opinion – and got it in no uncertain terms. I told her about the job offer and how I'd told them I'd think about it. I just wasn't sure. Brenda just stared at me and then almost gasped the words out. 'Are you for real? They've only gone and offered you the England job and you don't know if you should fucking take it? Are you insane? You ring and tell them you'll accept or I'll beat the living shit out of you!'

But I wasn't ready to say 'yes'. The following day, I went back to FA headquarters for more talks. I can't remember much of what we discussed, but I do recall we talked a fair amount about how to bring the younger players through. At the time, England had no youth system and young players were not being developed. In truth, the previous manager, Ted Copeland, had not just been sacked because England hadn't qualified for the World Cup. It was because we were a nation in fast decline. The gulf between us and the top world sides was becoming a chasm. The year before, we'd played the USA in two back-to-back friendlies and were hammered 5–0 and 6–0. In truth, we were humiliated. The FA realised that things had to change. So why not go radical and offer it to a 31-year-old with no management experience? My dream had always been to help professionalise women's football in England, to make us like Germany, France and the USA. So surely being offered this chance out of the blue was manna from heaven?

But I still wasn't sure. Going from being a player to becoming an international team manager in one go just seemed such a massive step. Yes, I had earned my coaching badges – I'd got the UEFA B licence at that point – and I knew the game really well. But was I a manager? Let alone an international manager?

I had to borrow a couple of business suits off Brenda, because I didn't want to return in my one and only interview number. This time, they wanted me to meet the big cheese himself, Howard Wilkinson. Kelly Simmons was there once again, and Kelly and Howard talked to me about development plans, budgets and upcoming games and training camps. If I accepted the offer, I would be responsible for overseeing the whole women's set-up: manage the senior international team and help reorganise grassroots football in the women's game. As job responsibilities go, it was a massive undertaking. But it was the England job.

I remained non-committal. It was really important for me that they should see that I would never be a pushover. You have to start as you mean to go on. Howard looked at me with a quizzical stare. Like Robin Russell in my first interview, I don't think he could believe I wasn't ripping his arm off. I asked them why they had asked me? Was I second, third or fourth choice? Who'd already turned them down? Because I never want to be second, third or fourth choice for anything. I don't know whether they were lying or not, but they said I was the first person they had asked. Which mystified me. I had never managed before. They told me I had a great track record, I thought deeply about the game. I'd spent 15 years in the England set-up and knew its strengths and its weaknesses. Howard asked me for a decision. I reminded him that I'd been given seven days to make my mind up, shook his hand and said I'd give them a definite 'yes' or 'no' by the end of the week. The look on his face said, 'Who is this bloody woman?'

The next day, Kelly Simmons rang me and said, 'You know what, Hope? If you don't take it, someone else will do the job. And you'll be sat in the dressing room, thinking you could have done it better.'

That hit me. It was the decider. After being threatened by Brenda, browbeaten by Michelle, and now with Kelly's words ringing in my ears, I rang them to accept. Despite it all feeling very scary and a total leap into the unknown, this was a once-in-a-lifetime opportunity. I had to do it. Being young, female and black I knew I could be a positive role model and wanted to succeed for everyone else as well as myself.

There was no question that they would let me be a player-manager. I would have far too much on my plate, and the steepest of learning curves to climb, so the deal was that I would stop playing pretty much immediately. They let me see out my last couple of games with Croydon and then I hung up my boots.

Or, more accurately, threw them to a little girl in the crowd after my final, final whistle blew. I didn't mourn it. I loved playing football more than anything in the world. But I was 31 and starting to think about life after playing. This gave me something that I had never expected.

So, in one fell swoop, England got its first black manager, its first woman manager, and its first gay manager. I told the FA from the off that I lived with my partner Michelle, just in case the press wanted to make any kind of issue about it. Refreshingly, they didn't. Overall, the press gave me a very enthusiastic welcome, albeit in the limited amount of column inches that women's football gained in those days.

It was one of the most surreal weeks of my life. I started it hoping to get a little bit of work with the FA in youth coaching, and fully expecting to play on as a footballer at Croydon for a few more years. Seven days later, I was England's first full-time professional manager – a soon-to-be-retired footballer, contemplating dramatic new changes in my life.

A few weeks later, I started my first day at Lancaster Gate. Surprise, surprise, I didn't get an office like Glenn Hoddle. I got a desk and the shared use of a PA, Helen Nicolaou. Gradually, Helen would become full-time with me, and thank God for that. She was brilliant at her job.

I was handed an FA American Express card and told I would get a company car. I talked to HR, signed my contract, and then sat back down at my little desk. I gazed around the room at paintings of old administrators and long forgotten men in suits, and wondered what the hell I was doing there. I was that little West Indian kid from Juniper Flats council estate in Peckham, who had posters of Kevin Keegan and Ray Wilkins on her bedroom wall and played footie with the boys. Now I was sat at my own desk, England manager, working for the oldest FA in the world. Then it dawned on me. This, I realised, is what you call progress. I knew my mum would be proud. That all my loved ones and friends would be made up. But I also realised it was a statement – to all people who came from backgrounds like me. That's why there was such an added reason for me to succeed in that job.

But one fact remained. What *do* you do as manager of the England women's football team, literally, on a day-to-day basis? It may seem bizarre, but everyone just seemed to assume that I knew what I was meant to be doing.

All I knew was that the first big project I had to organise was a talent identification camp for young and upcoming players from the 50-plus women's academies around the country. I had to talk to an army of coaches and get each of them to recommend their three best players and send them on the camp. The date and venue for the camp was already arranged. What I had to do was work out the logistics of the whole thing.

Not for the first time, I turned to my old mentor, Alan May. Right from the off, it was so important to have someone in there that I knew and trusted and could bounce ideas off. Not only did Alan help me sort the talent camp, he started giving me expert advice about people-management, time-management and how to run a team. He told me there would be a lot of politics involved in the job. Whether I liked it or not, I would have to learn how to deal with that.

Alan hardly ever praised me – that was his style. So I won't tell you here what an immense and supportive influence he has been for me throughout my entire career. Or how much he helped me to swim at the FA when, for a while, I felt I was sinking. He sat me down and got me to create a list of objectives, the main one being to get the full England national team into the top ten of European football.

There was no template to follow. I was the first full-time professional England manager and much of what went before had been achieved on a piecemeal basis by part-timers and volunteers. Somehow I had to pull all these different strands together and move everything from grassroots development upwards on to a more professional footing. It really was a blank sheet of paper. I had the help of a part-time assistant in Paul Smalley, who was a national coach and former pro-footballer with Notts County and Scunthorpe. I had Alan. And that was pretty much about it. I needed to grow my team.

Everything starts at the grassroots, and we identified a shake-up of the scouting system as crucial. We put together a network of 20 scouts across the country to help winkle out new talent and track the progress of existing players. It soon became patently clear that I needed more budget.

But first I had to gain everyone's trust at the FA. It was really important to me in those first few weeks that people saw me as approachable and diligent. But I also needed them to know that I didn't suffer fools gladly and would always speak my mind. If you don't want to hear the answer, then don't ask me the question. I said to myself, 'I'm not going to be intimidated.'

Howard Wilkinson had a reputation for being tough, ruthless. And when I started my 15 years as England manager, he wasn't at all convinced by women's football. He wasn't openly dismissive, just not particularly interested. I knew I had to get him to change his mind. A few days into my job I asked if I could call him 'Howie'.

He looked me up and down and couldn't help but smile. 'You can call me want you want.' I knew I'd charmed him. I also knew that within the FA he had a lot of clout. If I was really going to help women's football develop in England, I needed someone with clout on my side. I worked hard to gain his trust, showed him that I already knew a fair bit. What I didn't know, I was desperate to learn. Anything I could do that would gain me that extra one per cent, I wanted to learn. And still do.

I never called him Howie after that and always referred to him as Howard from then on in. It was a respect thing. Initially, I just wanted to get his attention – and I got it. To this day, Howard is one of my heroes. Highly intelligent, supportive and honest, he helped me more in the early days than anyone else at the FA. His reputation within the game is immense. Lest we forget, he was the last English manager to win the top division in 1992, the season before it became the Premier League.

As a player, he had a fairly modest career, playing as a winger for Brighton, Sheffield Wednesday and Boston United. But as a manager he was forward thinking and always looking at new ways to play the game. He was open-minded and always wanting to learn. I took a lot from that. After he left Leeds, in 1997 he was appointed FA technical director, in charge of overseeing coaching and training programmes at all levels of the game.

In the early days of the job, before the tournaments and friendlies began with the international squad, I had a lot of thumb-twiddling time at my little desk. One day Kelly Simmons asked me how it was going. I told her, 'To be honest, I don't have a lot to do.' She grinned very knowingly, and replied, 'Don't worry, Hope. You will have.' And she was bloody right ...

Chapter 7

The Desk in the Corner

Did the FA appoint me because I was black and a woman? Was it a tokenistic gesture? These thoughts ran through my mind once I'd accepted the job. There were people who said I wasn't qualified for the position. That I had no managerial experience. And to a great extent, they were right. But I did know women's football and the national squad inside out. That had been my world for the previous 15 years.

Whatever the reasons for my appointment, one thing was for sure. I really felt a responsibility to succeed. As the first black woman ever to manage an England national sports team, failure was never an option. I knew I would really have to work my arse off. But as I sat at my empty desk during that first week, one thought went through my mind over and over again. I had no idea what I was actually meant to do.

Sure, I knew that in the diary there was the talent identification event which I was responsible for organising. There was a fairly short fixture list of upcoming games but, beyond that, I didn't have a clue what I was meant to be doing on a day-to-day basis. Nobody in Lancaster Gate told me what I was meant to be doing. Everyone seemed to presume that I knew. In truth, I don't think anybody knew. In many ways, we were all making it up as we went along in those early days.

There was also the matter of getting to know new work colleagues and finding my way around the building. To be honest, in the beginning I felt a little bit like an alien who'd been beamed down into Lancaster Gate. I also think a lot of people there were a little scared of me. I think they found me a little ... 'God, who is she?' In truth, at the time, not a lot of them had much experience of working with black people in a position of power, and I am someone who has always tried to speak my mind. But I always try to treat people with utter respect, whoever they are. I don't believe in hierarchies and always attempt to deal with people as I would hope to be dealt with. And it cuts both ways. I will not allow anyone to treat me as subservient.

One day during my first week there, I was on the phone when FA coach Derek Fazackerley walked through. He took one look at me on the phone and asked, 'Is that the new girl?', assuming that all women are bloody secretaries. I put him straight.

Even Robin Russell, who I grew to really like, could be a little patronising in my early days at the FA. One day I was talking to one of the new FA regional directors, Steve Rutter, when Robin came into the room. He said 'hello' to Steve but didn't even acknowledge that I was standing there. Completely ignored me. I said to him, 'Do not look straight through me. Please show me the decency of saying hello to me as well.' From then on, we got on just fine.

From Robin, though, I did get some idea of how much attention was paid to women's football within the FA. He very helpfully advised me to pick the Arsenal back four for my first few international games. 'Great,' I said, 'even the Irish one?'

Apart from those guys, I had very little to do with the rest of the high-ups and suits. They pretty much left me alone, which was fine by me, but bizarre. I was the manager of the England women's team but during the time that Graham Kelly was chief executive, he didn't once as much as speak to me.

My first match in charge was a friendly against Sweden in July 1998 at Victoria Road, Dagenham. I inherited the same squad that up until a few weeks before I had been a part of. But going from player to manager wasn't a tough transition. I wasn't consumed in player life, not towards the end of my playing career. I was a bit of a loner, a bit remote. I had a couple of friends in the squad, but no one particularly special. Not like in my early days as an international. I had very strong opinions as a player, so that was nothing new to the rest of the squad when I became manager.

We lost the game 1–0. Standing on the touchline you get a totally different perspective of a team than when you're a player on the pitch, in the thick of it. We lost the game to a goal in the 84th minute to Swedish debutante Malin Moström. We were always conceding late goals. And watching from the sidelines it was blatantly obvious why. The players just weren't strong enough or fit enough, which was a worrying conclusion to reach, as our next match was against world champions Norway in Lillestrøm.

Back in those days, women's international teams were divided into two 'divisions' – the elite sides and then, in division two, the rest of the worst. We were in the elite group but only by the skin of our teeth. We lost 2–0 to Norway, which sent us bottom of our Euro qualifying group and put us into a two-legged relegation play-off against Romania. A lot was riding on the games. Had England lost, we would have been demoted to the B level and therefore unable to qualify for any of the major tournaments.

It would also have led to a substantial drop in funding, and totally sabotage my plans for developing the women's game. Thankfully, we won 6–2 on aggregate to stay in the top flight. I decided to start as I meant to go on, and had us playing a more fluid 4–3–3. Ted had demanded we play a much more direct game. But I felt that didn't get the best out of our more skilful players. Given what was at stake, the two games were nerve-racking for everyone. I was too busy trying to get everyone organised to be particularly nervous, but the nagging doubt at the back of my mind was we could lose our A-level status. The girls enjoyed the system, played well in both games and rightly beat an inferior Romanian team twice.

I realised that if we were ever going to compete against the likes of Germany and the United States, we had to become more professional in our approach, and that was particularly true of training and conditioning. We had to get fitter and stronger. So I hired people who would help us do that. Jill Chapman was our part-time physio, and I took on Louise Fawcett to join her full time. Jill had worked with Millwall, various top-flight rugby teams and the Royal Air Force and specialised in sporting injuries and conditions. Graham Keeley became my first goalkeeping coach and regional development manager. I brought Mo Marley in to work part-time with me on the under-19s. When I became confident in her – and her in herself – I left Mo to it. And key to the whole revolution, exercise scientist Dawn Scott and my chief medical officer Dr Pippa Bennett.

Dawn had a big interest in exploring what effects the physical demands and training loads had upon elite women footballers, not just in this country but, crucially, abroad. She was tasked with assessing the strength, agility and power of our players to look at ways we could improve their overall fitness through conditioning, different exercise strategies and nutrition. Dawn would be crucial in our aim to turn England players into full-on 90-plus minute performers. She drafted in a five-foot-nothing weightlifting champion and bodybuilder, Barry Beedsley. He designed the strength programme around weights, and aligned it specifically around the movements footballers made while playing. He was a great guy!

Pippa was a brilliant sports doctor who would become a firm friend. She was an expert in injury prevention, injury rehabilitation and maximising performance and, like Dawn, would bring a new scientific approach to how we worked with the players. I told everyone on the team that they had a clean sheet of paper to work on, and said, 'Now help me make everything better.'

Together, we set up individual training and conditioning programmes that really made a difference to the players. I asked Howard Wilkinson to help me get funding – I think it was around £50,000 – to set up regional centres where members of our squad could go to work locally with trainers and specialists on their programmes. Initially, we were asking them to do two conditioning sessions a week to bring their strength and conditioning up to the kind of levels you saw in the German players. Some of the players were resistant, saying they didn't want to start looking like muscle-bound men. You've got to bear in mind, too, that in those days all the women's clubs in England trained together, at most two times a week. We were asking for a lot more commitment; it was a big cultural change. But without it, we couldn't hope to compete at the top level. It was time for change in oh so many ways.

Of course, when I played for England, we'd turn up on a Friday night and then play the game on a Sunday. There was little time for the manager and the coaches to work with the players. Good foreign squads – many of whose players were professional or at least semi-professional – would get together for much longer before games. I established a routine where the squad would meet up for four days before a match. To help compensate them for time they had to take off work, the FA started to pay them a £400 weekly fee.

I looked at our fixture lists, past and present, and compared them to those of the top teams. When I took over, England were playing on average five times a year. Germany and the USA averaged 15 to 20 games per annum. Some of their players were on 120-plus caps and still a long way off the end of their careers. To improve, we had to play more games together. So I set about getting us more matches outside of the usual competitions and tournaments. If we were going to feel good, we had to look good. It may seem a little thing, but when I took over as manager our kit was basically the men's outfits. So I talked with the people at Umbro and got them to design women's shirts, the right size and the right cut. It was important for us to forge our own identity as women footballers, and having the right kit was a part of that.

I soon found, though, that the hardest part of being a manager was making tough decisions about players and staff. Suddenly you're making these big decisions that affect people's lives. My first one would concern the squad physiotherapist. She had been my physio as a player and I just didn't feel that she was particularly attentive, or right for what I needed, to take us forward on the fitness and conditioning front. So one of my first decisions was to get rid of her. It was agonising for me. I'd never been in a position where I was responsible for other people's careers, and the idea of letting someone go horrified me. But Alan drilled it into me that, as a manager, I would have to get used to this: it would happen many times in the future. I needed to develop strategies to deal with it. He continually preached that a manager has to be decisive.

But the physio beat me to it. The day I had planned to talk with her, her letter of resignation arrived on my desk. I would have had that conversation. But I was also relieved not to have to do it, so early in my tenure.

Within a couple of years I came to realise how unexpected events could blindside you as a manager and force you into situations where you had to make decisions fast, when you were least expecting them. Sammy Britton was a real character and, when I was an England player, a good friend. Her versatility made her a positive asset to the squad – Sammy could play anywhere, in defence, midfield or attack. In November 2000, Sammy admitted to taking marijuana prior to our second Euros play-off game against Ukraine. But, inexplicably, her routine drug test after the first leg came back negative. As England manager, I couldn't let this go. I felt it was important to send out a clear message to women's football that this type of behaviour was not acceptable, particularly from a top international player. I had no alternative but to suspend her. Cannabis was an illegal drug and I didn't want anyone who might pull on an England shirt to think I turned a blind eye to such transgressions.

To be honest, I was bloody annoyed with Sammy for putting me in that position. As an athlete and an experienced England international with over 40 caps, she shouldn't have been messing about with drugs. As a manager, I soon learnt that if you suddenly decide you have to leave a player out, you have to detach yourself from friendships. I drafted her back into the squad after she'd served a three-match international ban. But later on, in 2005, I dropped her from the England squad altogether and Sammy pretty much stopped speaking to me. That was sad. But as England manager, it was a decision I had to make.

Gillian Coultard was a legend in English women's football. At the time I took over as England manager, she was England's most honoured player with 119 caps. At club level, Gill won two National Team titles and six FA Women's Cup finals during 24 years with the Doncaster Belles. Joining them as a 13-year-old, she made over 300 appearances for the club that dominated English women's football for many a long year. But, in her mid-thirties, I felt she had gone past her best and I dropped her. She was not happy.

A little later down the line, I had to get rid of someone I'd worked with for a long time. Paul Smalley had been my part-time assistant but, after a while, Howard and the FA realised that my workload was too much. I really needed someone full-time. So Paul, along with a number of other applicants, had to go through the process of interview. But he didn't turn out to be the best candidate. Howard thought I was going to employ Paul full-time, but I didn't. When he asked me who I wanted to appoint, he was really shocked. He was happy to ring Paul to let him know the bad news. But I was adamant that I should take responsibility for making the decision.

I rang Paul and I'm really sad to say he didn't take it well. A lot of words were exchanged and, in the end, I had to put the phone down on him, and I said I'd continue to talk when he stopped being such a wanker. Eventually Paul forgave me and today we have a good friendship. But one thing is for sure – if you like to be liked, football management is not for you.

A year into my new job, the 1999 World Cup kicked off in America. Under previous manager Ted Copeland, England had failed to qualify and, in truth, we were well beaten in our group, losing five out of the six games. Albeit, we were up against two of Europe's best sides in Germany and Norway and, at that time, weren't in touching distance of the top sides. So though it was a disappointment not to make it to the party that was USA 1999, it wasn't unexpected. But to witness what happened out there was fantastic for everyone involved in the women's game. In 1999, it truly went global. Women's football – or 'soccer', as it's known in the States, of course – had never seen anything like it. The US press and media coverage was unprecedented. American players appeared on the *Late Show with David Letterman*. Major newspapers produced lavish Women's World Cup pull-outs. Shops the length and breadth of the nation sold souvenirs. USA captain Mia Hamm even had her own signature Barbie Doll. Spread all over the country, in some of the nation's biggest sporting venues, it was the single largest women's sporting event in the history of the world. All 32 matches were televised live by ESPN and the ABC Network, and over 40 million viewers tuned in to the final. In the grounds, even the group stage matches that featured foreign sides averaged crowds of 30,000. To watch their USA team, the fans turned out in legions. In the first semi-final, 73,000 watched the hosts beat Brazil 2–0 at the Stanford Stadium in California. It was played ahead of a major men's league match between DC United and San Jose. Before the men took to the pitch, an estimated 60,000 fans who'd just watched the women play upped and left.

The final at the Pasadena Rose Bowl, between the USA and China, was played out in front of 90,185 fans, which included

President Bill Clinton and a host of international celebrities and politicians. Goalless after extra-time, it was settled in a dramatic penalty shoot-out, with Brandi Chastain powering home the winning spot kick. The images of her pulling off her shirt, celebrating with her teammates and paying homage to the fans remain iconic for women's football to this day. The stadium – and most of America – went wild.

USA 1999 was a defining event in the history of women's sport in general, let alone of football. The huge interest it generated culminated two years later in the first major professional US women's league, the WSL.

A number of bigwigs from the FA attended the 1999 tournament, but I was never asked if I needed to go and have a good look at the best women's football could offer. At the time I didn't think anything of it. I was new to the job, I never gave it a second thought. It was only in hindsight that I began to think what a dumb decision that was. I really should have been sent to the USA World Cup. It would have been a vital opportunity to check out other nations, look at how they prepared and played; observe how their coaches set about directing them from the touchline, and get a feel for top tournament football. But the fact remains, the FA never sent the England Women's football manager to the Women's football World Cup in 1999. What I saw I watched on the telly. And what I saw convinced me that a sea change was happening right in front of my eyes. Women footballers were playing in front of huge crowds on national TV at peak time, albeit it in America. This was a landmark for the tournament globally. Now we had to get more people in England keen on the game. To do that, we needed to become winners on the pitch.

Chapter 8

On to 2001

My main task on the pitch was to get us qualified for the 2001 Euros in Germany. We'd been drawn in the same group as twice winners Norway, Portugal and Switzerland. The group winners qualified outright, while second and third placed went forward into a round of two-legged play-offs.

We were more than capable of taking Portugal and Switzerland out of the equation, but knew that Norway would be formidable opponents. We managed to beat Portugal 2–0 at Barnsley's Oakwell ground. But not before we got some expert advice. At the time, my childhood hero Kevin Keegan was the England men's manager. We had the occasional chat when he was in at Lancaster Gate and, just before the Portugal game, he offered to come in and take a coaching session. I was absolutely thrilled. This was the guy whose pictures used to be on my bedroom wall, and he was coming in to help coach the England women! The players couldn't believe it either – twice European Footballer of the Year and all-round England legend taking them out on to the training field.

Kevin was a lovely guy and had no airs or graces. He spent a couple of hours with us out on the pitch, put the girls through their paces, and showed everyone he'd lost none of his touch on the ball. It was a great boost for us before the Portugal game.

Over the years, Kevin was the England men's manager I had most contact with at FA headquarters. By the very nature of the men's job, where their sole responsibility was to look after the senior side, not many of the managers spent much time at the FA. Roy Hodgson got me involved in a couple of his England training sessions, and I talked tactics sometimes with Fabio Capello. But, overall, I mixed very little with the string of managers who came and went.

After we played Portugal, I drove home with Michelle and some friends who came to see the game. My mobile rang and because I was behind the wheel, Michelle answered for me. The voice at the other end said, 'Hello, it's Kevin.' 'Kevin who?' Michelle replied. 'Is that Hope?' With her face and eyes beaming, Michelle mouthed the words, 'It's Kevin Keegan!' Everyone in the car had their fists in their mouths trying to stop themselves from screaming out loud as I took the call. He was really sweet, asking how the game had gone and wishing us the best in the rest of the group games. We must have talked for two or three minutes, and Kevin said if there was anything else I needed, just to give him a ring. Then he rang off, and everyone in the car started screaming, hollering and laughing. 'Kevin Keegan! You've been rung by Kevin Keegan.' Everyone found it so funny.

Later in the year, we travelled to Portugal for the away game and got a hard-fought 2–2 draw. Over the two ties we beat Switzerland 3–0 away and 1–0 at home, but at Norwich City's Carrow Road Norway won 3–0 and though my players put in a gutsy, committed performance, the Norwegians never really had to move out of the lower gears. We went to Norway for the away fixture and got absolutely hammered 8–0 – still our record defeat at international level. Norway were on fire. But, ridiculous though this may sound, it was the one game out of the group that gave me the most hope for the future. I had fielded four young players – Kelly Smith, Rachel Yankey, Rachel Brown and Katie Chapman – all of whom, despite the drubbing, never let their heads go down.

The Norwegians were two up within 17 minutes and four up at half-time. They were an irresistible force. But my four new players continued to battle and fight and do the things I had asked them to do. I wanted players coming through who bought into what I was trying to achieve and I saw something special in Yankey, Smith, Brown and Chapman that night. The quartet would, of course, go on to become ever-presents in my England teams.

Our results against Portugal and Switzerland left us runners-up in the group, which meant a two-legged play-off against Ukraine for a place in the 2001 Euros tournament proper. We travelled to Boryspil for the first leg on 30 October 2000 and travelled home as 2–1 winners. A month later we notched up a 2–0 win at Leyton Orient's Brisbane Road. The exciting thing for the girls was 7,102 paying fans turned up to watch, which was a new record for an England women's international. The crowd was one of the loudest we'd ever played in front of – they roared us on from start to finish. It was exhilarating to stand on the touchlines and experience such enthusiastic backing for an England women's match. To be honest, back in 2000, we weren't used to such support. It was fitting that we should reward the crowd with a win that would take us through to the Euros.

We did not travel to Germany with many expectations, but we did travel first class. The marketing people really pulled out the stops and got the FA to pay for a chartered flight from Luton Airport, there and back, and pushed for us to get our own coach to take us to and from matches and training. They were trying to get the UK press and media to see that we should be taken seriously but, sadly, it had little impact on our press coverage for 2001. Our presence in Germany hardly gained footnotes in the mainstream newspapers, let alone TV or radio.

I didn't really expect us to get through the group stage, as all the other teams in the tournament were way ahead of us, and for good reason. Our players still only trained twice a week. Sweden and Germany's women, for example, trained ten times a week. They undertook regular conditioning and weights programmes. We didn't – yet. But myself and the team were working on it. Most of the other major European nations had their own highly developed semi-professional leagues that played to high standards. In 2001, we were just introducing our first national league. We were so far behind it was untrue.

My first tournament squad was a mix of older players like Pauline Cope, my captain Mo Marley (who would later become the under-19 coach), Marieanne Spacey and Karen Walker, and youngsters making their way into the senior side like Rachel Unitt and Katie Chapman, who were both 19, and a 20-year-old Rachel Brown.

It was a sign of the times that we had three players in the squad from the newly set up American Women's League – Browny, who kept goal for Pittsburgh Panthers; a 22-year-old Kelly Smith who was playing for the Philadelphia Charge; and 20-year-old Danielle Murphy who was a defender at the Florida Gators. Nearly half of the 20-player squad turned out for Doncaster Rovers and Arsenal, which reflected their continuing dominance in the domestic game at the time.

So, off to Germany. For all three of our group games – against Russia, Sweden and Germany – we were based in Jena, an old university town that was a world centre for the optical industry. So we were hoping for some good refereeing! Before the fall of the Berlin Wall, Jena had been part of the old East Germany, and still had the feeling of trying to get itself up to speed as a non-communist city.

It was marvellous to get to the tournament, but it was always going to be a big ask to get out of the group stage. We were still very much a work in progress, and while Germany and Sweden were among the tournament favourites, the Russians were a tough, physical squad with a lot of experience. I knew they would pose us a lot of problems. They also came into the tournament as group winners, having won all six of their qualifiers. The Russians would be our first opponents at the Ernst-Abbe-Sportfeld in Jena, which would be our home for all three of the group matches. It was the base of FC Carl Zeiss Jena and had recently been rebuilt. The stands were modern and the facilities at the ground impressive. If we had any chance of progressing then a win against Russia was a must.

The young Kelly Smith had been showing great promise in an England shirt and I wanted to start her against Russia. She already had such power and pace, and was a great decision maker on the pitch. A natural. But she picked up an ankle injury in training and was replaced by the albeit hugely experienced Marieanne Spacey.

As we'd expected, the Russians played with a smothering back five and were big, strong and physical. They pushed us back for the first half-hour or so, though we did carve out a string of half chances. It looked even-stevens for half-time, until Angela Banks pounced on to a ball just inside Russia's box and drilled a shot home to put us one up at the break.

Russia came out like a train in the second half and our goalie Pauline Cope was forced into a string of fine saves. Finally their pressure told and, on 62 minutes, Alexandra Svetlitskaya burst into the box and slotted home what was in all truth a deserved equaliser. It ended 1–1, and then the hard work really began.

Our next two group games ended up as a cruise for Germany and Sweden. My players showed a lot of guts and determination and ran themselves into the ground. But our far superior opponents were so strong, fit and athletic they both won at a canter. Germany beat us 3–0, Sweden 4–0. So we finished the group in bottom place with a solitary point, having scored just the one goal and conceding eight. A telling statistic was that six of those were conceded in the last 30 minutes of each of the three games. Although we'd made leaps and bounds in trying to improve the fitness and conditioning of the players, we were still behind the better teams. But the 2001 Euros in Germany were always going to be a learning curve for us. Getting there had been an achievement and what the players needed more than anything was tournament experience: one game after another, in quick succession. A few of the squad like Pauline Cope, Marieanne Spacey, Mary Phillip, Julie Fletcher and Becky Easton had played alongside me in the 1995 World Cup. But for the youngsters coming in, it was all new. If these young players were going to form our future, it was vital that they gained as much tournament nous as possible. And the more we played together, the better we would become.

After we came home from Germany, I pressed for more friendly games, which at first the powers that be were reluctant about. But with support from Howard, more budget and logistics were made available to help us play more as a national side, even if, in my early days as manager, most of those friendlies – of which we played a good few – were behind closed doors.

If, say, we had a friendly against the USA, I would ask the USA (or whoever the potential opposition were), if we could play them in front of a crowd. Then maybe the following day give them a game behind closed doors as well. It gave other squad players experience of playing against the best, and didn't really cost the FA much. With no crowd, we didn't need groundstaff or stewards. So we only had to pay for the hire of the stadiums.

You only improve if you get to play the best international sides, and if you're not a regular in the major tournaments … well, I had to find another way of pitting ourselves against the leading nations. It was important for all of my senior players to understand what was required, to get themselves on to the next level.

The Euros had been an eye-opener for a lot of the younger players, who weren't perhaps aware of just how far ahead the best teams were in terms of strength, fitness and match mentality. I think some of the players were shocked by both Germany and Sweden – how easily they were both able to manage and dictate the pace in their games against us, and, basically, just stay in cruise control. We had a lot of very skilled, talented performers who were coming through. But they needed these big match experiences to understand how much they needed to advance.

Off the pitch, we were slowly piecing together a plan that would revolutionise the way that English women's football operated. The team I was beginning to gather around me had an immense influence on all of that. Together, we introduced new youth teams, under-21s, under-19s and under-17s, so there would be a clear pathway for young players to follow if they had the ability to play at the top level. Later, we would introduce an under-15 level.

Before I became manager there was no national youth system, zilch. Young players weren't gradually introduced to international football but thrown straight in at the deep end with the seniors. It didn't take a genius to realise that this was severely holding back the development of the game in England. Again, we were light years behind the top nations, who all had well-established age-level squads rising from under-15s through to their senior squads.

I was particularly keen to get the under-15s going, to help retain the interest and ambition of girls who were no longer able to play in their school teams. The plan was that the under-15s would meet regularly for regional training camps, and eventually those camps would travel abroad, to give young players an early introduction to international exposure.

Although I had overall responsibility for each of the age levels, my old captain, Mo Marley, who was gaining a fine reputation as a coach, was put in charge of the under-19s once we had the system up and running. I have been close to Mo for many years, and one of the toughest jobs I had to do was to tell her it was time to retire as a player. It comes to us all, but it's hard for footballers to make the decision. Many play on well beyond their sell-by date, both men and women, because they love to play the game – for all of their young lives it's all they've known.

What Mo had, and it's what I told her, was massive potential as a coach. She understood the game, was always thoughtful on the pitch as a player, and I encouraged her to draw a veil on her playing career to get involved in coaching. At first, it terrified the life out of her. I asked her to take some sessions with the England youth teams, and she just didn't want to do it. But Mo was cajoled into giving it a go, and the rest is history. Lois Fidler would later be appointed under-17 manager, and Brent Hills would take over the under-23s, which was launched further on, in 2004, to put us in line with the leading nations in women's football globally.

I asked that all the different age levels – except the under-15s – play in a 4–3–3 formation. The theory being that players would find the rise to the next age level more straightforward if they were already comfortable playing within that system. For the under-15s, I was more concerned that first they were introduced to 4–4–2 as the basic foundation, and to develop them tactically. 4–3–3 is a flexible and fluid set-up that allows players to contribute to every phase of play. Students of the game will know that it was first popularised by Brazil in the 1962 World Cup and was a development on the 4–2–4 system that had been pretty much universal before then. Generally speaking, what's good for the Brazilians is pretty much good for everyone else.

4–3–3 is all about energy and being expansive: full-backs who are prepared to bomb forward and overlap the wingers, but also forge back at pace to defend their own by-line if necessary; an anchor midfielder who'll help shield the defence and be a first point of contact for moving the ball forward from her centre-backs. (Fara Williams has always epitomised that role.) In front of that anchor are two midfielders who are prepared to cover long hard miles in a match, moving back and forth, potentially being involved in every single move and/or playing just behind the Kelly Smiths of this world, the focal point of the attack. The forward works with two wingers, and the full-backs when they're on the attack, and, in turn, with the two central midfielders when they're going forward. Equally, a team that plays 4–3–3 can also quickly revert to a 4–5–1 if you need two of your three forwards to track back more into midfield.

I felt the system was easy to modify, as and when required. And obviously the secret to making any system work is to be ready to change and bend the basics of it depending on the game situation and whether your team is getting enough of the ball.

Since 1962, it's a formation that has served a lot of great sides very well. West Germany won the World Cup playing 4–3–3 in 1974, as did two-time finalists Argentina in 1974 and 1978. Johan Cruyff's Ajax team won three European Cups in the 1970s playing a 4–3–3; Chelsea used the formation during José Mourinho's first spell at Stamford Bridge.

I'm not saying that 4–3–3 is the template for everything, but it's a good start. Of course, there would sometimes be the necessity to play in a different formation because of sending offs, injuries or simply the very specific style of an opponent. But, by and large, I wanted players who were comfortable playing in one particular system, along one pathway through the under-17, under-19 and under-23 to the senior squads.

In 2001, I helped launch a major new FA initiative at Loughborough University, the National Player Development Centre. The academy was launched as the first ever university-level scheme in this country, aimed at coaching, supporting and helping young women footballers. The deal was that every year up to 20 young players would get backing from the FA to take part in a fully funded three-year scholarship. They would learn about everything from sports psychology and life management as a footballer to nutrition and a host of different toning, fitness and training theories. Over the years, it would produce players like

Casey Stoney, Karen Carney and Amanda Barr. I was put in charge of the project.

For England, this was truly groundbreaking and an indication of the women's game moving forward within the FA. But don't be under any illusions: there were still those at Lancaster Gate who just couldn't understand why 'ladies' would want to play football. Equally though, there were enough people within the organisation who realised the world was changing.

At grassroots level, we were playing catch-up to get a system in place that would help girls who liked football to get involved. My own experience of being told I was banned from playing for the school team, had given me first-hand experience of how tough it was for girls to find like minds, a team, a league even. I was lucky to find Millwall Lionesses and benefit from their pioneering approach to developing and coaching girls. But little had changed since I was 12. In 2002, a Sport England survey showed that only 13 per cent of girls had access to football coaching in their PE lessons, yet football was the sport of choice for girls. Strategy research at the FA revealed that 331,000 girls who played kickabout football wanted to join a team. We needed to help them.

Over the next few years, the FA began to work closely with schools around the country to develop more football coaching opportunities within their PE lessons and in after-school clubs, supported by FA Education Officers. Teachers were encouraged to study for FA curriculum-related qualifications, and schools were given access to equipment. Primary school girls were encouraged to play mini-soccer, with short games being played on small pitches with small goals. The FA School–Club Link was created to help develop sustainable relationships between schools and local clubs: the idea was to provide a clear route for young girls who wanted to continue their participation in football. The FA encouraged and supported schools competitions, leagues and festivals for both primary and secondary schoolgirls. The bottom line was: we wanted to make young girls realise that if they wanted to play football, we would do everything we could to make it happen. It was all about creating maximum participation opportunities for girls who loved football, no matter what their skill level. So far as I'm concerned, football is the greatest game in the world, and it doesn't matter how good you may be, every woman and girl should have the opportunity to play it at any and every level. In England, for so many decades, they had been denied this.

If girls with talent and commitment wanted to take their footballing lives further, we needed to give them opportunities to progress up the ladder, once they'd found a local club to play in. So the FA created over 50 licensed Centres of Excellence across England. The centres provided weekly quality coaching for each area's most promising girls, along with a fixture programme against the talented players at surrounding Centres of Excellence. Each centre was attached to a county FA, a county sports partnership or a professional men's team. The FA provided the money to keep each centre running.

It all added up to a massive commitment from the FA. None of these developments happened overnight, and it took time to put these systems in place. Across the country, an army of teachers, coaches, parents and enthusiasts helped turn them into reality. These are the unsung heroes and heroines who regularly, every week, put in countless hours of time, energy and passionate commitment – rainy January evenings, Sundays when they'd rather have stayed in bed, and long journeys back from away matches late at night. Over the years, I've met and worked with many of them. Forget the arguments about over-paid male footballers, the so-called stars and the money culture. These people are for me, what makes football the greatest game. The people's game.

Credit here must also be given to some of the great colleagues I worked with at the FA over the years: Rachel Pavlou, Ros Potts, Donna McIvor, Lucy Wellings and Helen Croft, who all made a massive contribution to developing the women's game. Their job was to be the feet on the ground, establish and organise the new Centres of Excellence, and co-ordinate the growth of the game in counties the length and breadth of the country. They helped county associations implement any new plans that came out of the FA, and did endless legwork at the grassroots level.

So the FA was really getting its act together to develop women's football. Now we needed to kick on and, although I had a lot on my plate that I was responsible for, I was a woman in a hurry. I could see how much had to be done – but also how much could be achieved. In 2002, we were handed an opportunity that would help us all hugely.

UEFA announced that England had been selected to host the 2005 European Championships. The Women's Committee at the FA had been keen to put in a bid. The chief executive at the time asked for my thoughts about trying to get the tournament in England. I told him if he thought we were going to win it, absolutely not. If he thought it would help grow the game, then absolutely yes. Fortunately, he went for the latter. So I said, 'Fine. Let's put in a bid to host it.'

I was overjoyed, as indeed were the rest of my team of staff and the players, when word came through that we'd been selected. It was a big fillip to women's football in this country to know that we would be hosting a major international tournament. The FA had worked really hard on putting together an excellent bid, with Helen Nicolaou and Lindsey Jackson at the forefront of the process. The rest of the UEFA nations clearly realised that what we were trying to achieve in England was a project worth supporting. This would not only be the first major women's football tournament ever to be played in England, but the very first tournament in women's sport in general. It would be a great showcase for what was being achieved in English women's football.

We had three years to prepare and, as hosts, would not have to play any qualifying group matches. This was equally a blessing and a curse. It would mean I could handpick opponents for a long string of friendlies to fine-tune us towards the tournament. But no matter how competitive I might have wanted my players to be, a friendly is not a tournament match.

In those early years at the FA, I was married to the job. I knew that all eyes were on me and, in a situation which I guess is not uncommon to most women working in a predominantly male environment, there were some people there who were willing me to fail. So I made sure that I always went that extra mile. I felt I had to keep proving myself over and over again. So life was exhausting: I had little time for socialising, and everything I did seemed to be in some way associated with work.

I was also beginning to realise what effect being in the public spotlight has upon your life. In 2004, Michelle and I bought a sandwich shop at the Bethnal Green end of Hackney Road in east London, which Michelle would run. On her grand opening day, one of the staff was unable to come in for work, so I volunteered my services. I cooked the bacon, helped make sandwiches, did the washing up – and, unfortunately, brought the shop to a virtual standstill.

The problem was people were coming in for sandwiches but as soon as they recognised me, wanted to stop to chat, take photos and have me autograph their shirts and suchlike. What was the England manager doing working behind the counter of a sandwich shop? Rather than a help, I became a total hindrance – particularly at peak lunchtime when the customers were in a queue that stretched out on to the street. Michelle and I decided that, in future, perhaps it wasn't such a great idea for me to help out at the shop. My short career as sandwich shop assistant came to a premature end.

I'm quite a private person and have never been comfortable being the centre of attention. But whether I liked it or not, being England manager turned me into public property so far as many other people were concerned. I was, of course, eager for women's football in England to get more publicity and coverage, and so from that point of view rarely turned down an interview or a photo opportunity.

With fans, I am always respectful, and wherever humanly possible will always sign autographs or have my picture taken with someone. Although, sometimes it can become a little too much. Michelle and I were sat with friends in a local restaurant one evening and, while we were eating and chatting, we became aware of a man pointing at us and talking to his friends. He walked over, completely butted into our conversation, introduced himself and sat down at our table, giving his footballing opinions about this and that. A few minutes later, to our relief, he got up and returned to his table. But he wasn't done just yet. He literally returned to our table with his own plate of food, sat back down next to us again and continued to hold forth.

I really don't crave the spotlight and would much rather go unnoticed. One Saturday, Michelle and I needed to buy a new telephone, so we jumped in the car and went to the local Currys store. When we walked into the shop, all heads turned. People began to point and I soon realised that everyone was looking at me. Then I realised why. There I was, on every single TV screen in the store, being interviewed on *Football Focus* – a hundred Hope Powells looking back at me. I just couldn't take it, grabbed Michelle's arm and made for the door. Michelle was like, 'But we need a new phone!' I told her we'd go to the Carphone Warehouse, wherever – anywhere but Currys!

It's amazing, too, how you get judged by people who don't actually know you from Adam. I was once shopping in Sainsbury's when a young girl came up to me and, very disapprovingly, said, 'You wouldn't see Steve McLaren doing the shopping.' I laughed and replied, 'I'm not him. And need to eat!'

Another time, when I was away with England, Michelle was doing some gardening at our house. A coach pulled up over the other side of the road. Thirty women and girls got out. It wasn't unusual to see crowds of people on our street – Nunhead Cemetery is very nearby and it's almost as big and historic as the more famous Highgate Cemetery, where everyone from Karl Marx to Malcolm McLaren, Douglas Adams and Jeremy Beadle are buried. So we were both used to people arriving for tours of the cemetery, or big family visits to honour their deceased loved ones. But then the group of women walked determinedly over to Michelle and asked if this was where Hope Powell lived. Nonplussed, she said that I wasn't home and, feeling a little unnerved, went back inside the house. They stayed outside our home for a good 15 minutes, taking photos of the house and of one another, and then drove off. It was like one of those LA celebrity coach tours you read about. They weren't in any way aggressive or intimidating towards Michelle, but it was bizarre.

Believe me, I have never remotely wanted to be a celebrity, whatever that is. But hard though it may sometimes be, if you're in a high-profile job that's in the public eye, whether you like it or not, you're going to be recognised. I guess it's also proof that the women's game is getting more coverage and column inches. From the outset, that's what I wanted.

Chapter 9

Pro Licence

I'd started to gain my coaching qualifications early, passing the FA's preliminary coaching badge when I was 18, which helped me to get work throughout my twenties coaching football in the community. I was a sports development officer for Lewisham Borough Council and in Crystal Palace FC's community outreach scheme. Both of which gave me hundreds of hours of hands-on coaching experience with children and young people. My ex-England manager Ted Copeland had encouraged me to enrol in the FA's coach mentoring scheme, and from there I got my B licence while still playing.

Soon after I got the England manager's job, the FA asked me to take the A licence, the next qualification up. I'd wanted to take it ever since I'd passed my B but, to be honest, there was no way I could afford to pay for it myself. These things cost thousands of pounds, and that's a major obstacle for a lot of women wanting to get into coaching. This time, the FA were paying, thank goodness.

I received all the bumf through the post and showed it to Alan May. There was a list of the other coaches who would be on the course – all men – and they were variously at Arsenal's academy or Manchester United's, Chelsea's or Liverpool's, and I told Alan I had a bit of trepidation about doing the course. I knew I would be one of very few women on the course. And that turned out to be the case: the FA's Julie Chipchase was the only other woman on the course. Alan assured me that I'd be surprised at how much I already knew – and how little some of those academy coaches at Premier League clubs didn't. He was right. The first few presentations I watched on that course, which was held over two weeks at the FA's Lilleshall base, frankly underwhelmed me. In the end, it shouldn't be a gender issue. You're either a potentially good coach, or you're not. Not for the first time Alan was right, damn him.

But it was hard work. The difference between a B licence and an A licence was massive. The approach was very scientific – both in the classroom and, more importantly, out on the training pitch. The instructors included FA coaching director Dick Bate, future QPR manager Chris Ramsey and Steve Rutter, who would later become my assistant. They were great teachers, but it was a big learning curve.

We were shown how to develop senior players and teams. There were sessions on how to motivate players. A wide range of game play tactics and strategies were discussed, as well as looking at sports psychology, training session management and delivery, and match analysis. We looked at the angles of a run, the speed and timing of runs, how to form triangles with other players.

Everything happens so fast in a game that you really have to learn how to train your eye, so that you're not missing anything out there on the pitch. You've got to watch the player on the ball and what they're doing – while also being equally aware of all the other players off the ball, how they're positioning themselves, what runs they're looking to make, which areas of the pitch they're managing to find space in. It was bloody hard work, and a few on the course fell by the wayside.

For me, personally, I had to overcome the fact that I had suddenly become invisible. Whenever I put my hand up in the tutorials, I was never picked to answer. We were out on the training pitch doing a series of coaching exercises. Six times I put my hand up to volunteer for a task, and six times I was overlooked. I just couldn't get that old James Brown classic 'It's A Man's World' out of my head! I'm sure Julie felt the same.

Eventually, the men were tired, knackered out and didn't want to volunteer for any more practicals. I got my chance. It was only when the men saw me actually play football that I started to be given some grudging respect. I was fortunate that, having only just hung up my boots, I was still very fit and outdid a lot of the blokes on the course for stamina and fitness. Eventually, I gained my A licence, and I thought that was that.

But then, one morning in 2001, Howard arrived at my desk and pretty much told me I had to take the pro licence qualification. With the A now under my belt, Howard wanted me to go the whole way. The pro licence is football's top coaching qualification and broadly deals with advanced coaching, management skills and admin. It's aimed at Europe's elite band of coaches – and no woman had ever gained it before.

I said to Howard, 'Do I really have to? It's not like I don't have dozens of things on my plate right now.'

But he insisted, and I'm glad he did. Howard is a very clever man. He knew for sure that taking the pro licence would add to my skill set and experience. Howard also realised that by becoming the first woman in England to (hopefully) pass the qualification it would put down an important marker for the women's game, and help the disbelievers to take us all more seriously. As time went by, Howard had become not only more interested in the women's game, but a big supporter. He increasingly understood that women were utterly serious about wanting to professionalise their sport. Howard was a great ally.

But I'll be honest, I wasn't particularly looking forward to it. My experiences of taking all my previous badges had been depressingly the same. For my prelim badge, there was me and 20 men. Like the guys on the later A licence course, they couldn't get their heads around the idea of a woman being on the course with them, and I had pretty much been ignored there too. I'm quite a shy person at heart, and the idea of putting myself in this position again for the pro licence, knowing I would be the only woman on the course again, was daunting. I knew that, yet again, I would have to prove myself far more than any of the men on the course.

It was a massive commitment, too. Over 200 hours of contact time, a course at Warwick University, video conferences, plus countless essays, reports and coaching dossiers to write, and all over one single year. It kicked off with the ten-day course at Warwick, led by Howard and his assistant Les Reed. My fellow 'students' included Sammy Lee, Stuart Pearce, Phil Brown and Derek Fazackerley, then at Manchester City. The participants were split up into teams of four, and I shared my group with Sammy Lee, Steve Cotterill and Stuart Gray. I remember sitting down with them all for the first time and feeling very apprehensive. We were all football people, but the three of them all came from a different culture. All former players, their lives had been led in macho male dressing rooms. How would they view me, this woman in the midst of their training course?

I needn't have worried. Sammy, Steve and Stuart were welcoming, thoughtful and curious to know more about women's football. They were lovely guys to be with and we soon learnt to work well together as a team and share a lot of banter.

One of the first things we had to do was deliver a presentation together, showing how we would lead a coaching session for a specific Premier League game, West Ham v Liverpool, and then deliver it together as though it were to the players. Stuart Gray was appointed group leader. I'd taught myself how to do Power Point presentations, so volunteered to put ours together. Stuart then delivered it to the rest of that year's intake. It went down well, but not without some teething troubles in getting it together in the first place.

I remember Steve, Sammy, Stuart and myself met at 10 p.m. one night to work out the presentation. When those guys got together to talk about football they went gloriously off at tangents, remembering players' past performances, old matches and anecdotes from their own playing careers. An hour later, we'd got nowhere and I had to play head girl and get them focused: 'Guys, we still haven't put this together. Let's just concentrate on the nuts and bolts of how we're going to actually present this session.' And into the wee small hours we went.

Once we'd delivered our presentation, we had to put the planning into practice out on the training pitch, using young players from a local academy. I volunteered to lead the session, because I wanted to prove as publically as I could to any doubters that a woman could coach just as well as a man. And unlike my experiences of trying to volunteer for tasks on the A licence course, this time around I was very forceful and vocal about wanting to lead our team. So I put our presentation plan into practice and it worked out well.

One of the other guys on the course who I sensed was a doubter was Derek Fazackerley, who came up to me after the session and said in a back-handed kind of way, 'So women *can* coach.' I told him he shouldn't be so surprised. The other guys in my team were really complimentary, as was Howard. He made me laugh, because I had used an approach I always did in coaching to get the attention of the players quickly when I wanted to recreate a move. I would shout, 'Stop! Stand still! Don't move.' And it always had the desired effect. Then I would take them through the move again. Howard wondered where I'd picked that up from. 'From you, some years ago,' I told him.

By the end of the two weeks, our group was judged the best on the course. To this day, I still look out for what Sammy, Steve and Stuart's teams are doing and follow their careers.

Over the next year, I had to prove my competency in a number of different practical areas. A lot of this was essentially problem-solving. You would be given a 'what if' scenario. An example might be: 'One of your central defenders gets sent off after five minutes. How do you set about reorganising your tactics?' Sometimes you would deliver your analyses in a video conference, other times in an essay. It taught you how to become decisive during a game, sharpened the way you viewed the changing shape of a match.

Along the way, I attended numerous talks and tutorials. The wonderful Bobby Robson gave us a lecture-cum-chat, and he was amazingly inspirational. He was meant to talk and take part in a Q and A that lasted roughly an hour. Bobby was so passionate about football that two hours on he was still talking, arguing, asking for opinions and enjoying the craic of communicating with other football people.

I was also asked to show evidence that I was building on my interpersonal skills and actively improving my general coaching skills. Alongside all of the responsibilities I had to attend to at the FA, it meant a lot of midnight oil was burned throughout that year. The support of Michelle and my family and friends was, as ever, vital in helping me achieve all of this without going bonkers.

I was so proud to become the first woman to gain the first pro licence in England, and was glad that Mo Marley and Lois Fidler followed me in gaining the qualification soon afterwards. Other women have since passed, many others are preparing to study for it. The more of us who succeed, the more seriously the women's game is taken. In studying for the qualification alongside men, we're all operating on a level playing field and are judged in the same way. There's no tokenism at work. You're either a good, competent coach and pass, or you aren't and fail. So can women coach as well as men? Of course they bloody can.

I enjoyed the challenge of getting all of my badges. I've always valued learning – right back at Abbey Wood School I realised how important education is. It should be a lifetime process for everyone. We stop learning, we stand still. When I was 23 years old I gained a degree in sports science and history at the West London Institute of Higher Education. I learnt a lot there about study techniques, how to structure essays and so forth. That held me in really good stead for all the studying I had to do for my badges.

More recently, I've been in discussions to help implement some learning modules in sports science at the University of East London. It's still a work in progress, but, fingers crossed, I'll be more involved with that. A coach is, in many ways, like a teacher, and there's nothing more satisfying than passing on skills and then seeing students or players putting them into practice.

I've also been involved in the development of a unique new degree at Anglia Ruskin University, aimed at footballers who are coming to the end of their playing careers, the BSc (Hons) Coaching for Performance in Football. It's a distance-learning course that equips players with coaching and sports science skills to help prepare them for future work in the game. The university consulted with me to help shape the content of the course so that it was applicable to both male and female players. I think this degree is so important, because footballers really do need to seriously consider what they're going to do with their lives after their playing days are over. And so far as I'm concerned, while they are still playing, an educated player off the pitch makes a better player on the pitch.

I finally gained my pro licence in 2002, and continued to grow a brilliant working relationship with Howard. But in October of that year, I got some news that devastated me. Howard was leaving his role as FA technical director to go back into football management at Sunderland. I thought he was mad – off to a hiding to nothing at the Stadium of Light. More than anything, I would miss having him as my 'boss'. Howard had been one of the biggest influences on my life, and not to have him at the FA as my mentor and supporter filled me with dread. I got on really well with his deputy, and soon to be successor, Les Reed, but for me Howard was 'the special one'.

I also thought he was nuts to want to go back into management because he was doing such a great job at the FA as an agent of change. I was so sad for Howard that things turned out the way they did at the Stadium of Light. Sunderland was a club in free fall. Despite teaming up with my old pro licence buddy Steve Cotterill (his assistant), Howard couldn't check the Black Cats' slide into the Championship. Sunderland were a struggling team, way beyond repair, and Howard won only two games out of 20. They ended the season rock bottom with a then league history worst total of 19 points. In one home game against Charlton they managed to lose 3–1 by scoring three own goals inside seven minutes. Howard would go on to coach in China for a few short months, but it was not a fitting way for such a good manager to end his career in the hot seat.

In retrospect I could understand his decision to take on the Sunderland job as Howard is a man who thrives on new challenges. But it was a sad final chapter in management. Happily, Howard would go on to take the helm at the League Managers Association. It would have been a tragedy if such experience, wisdom and knowledge had been lost to football.

Howard's successor Les Reed was a lovely guy and had always been very supportive towards me. But it wasn't the same as the time I spent working with Howard. I mean no disrespect to Les in saying that, because we worked well together and he was a talented individual. But Howard had been my first, and vital, supporter at the FA when I arrived naïve, callow and unsure about what my position involved. He helped me so much in making my ideas and plans actually happen.

But life went on. Hard work continued on growing the age levels and grassroots side of the women's game, and my days continued to be long. However, for one day, all work was put on hold.

I travelled up to Preston, to join the likes of Sir Stanley Matthews, Eric Cantona, Sir Bobby Charlton and Bobby Moore and was inducted into the English Football Hall of Fame. I was extremely proud to become only the second woman inductee, following in the footsteps of the legendary Lily Parr. She had been named in the Hall of Fame the year before, when it had first been set up. It's important for anyone with an interest in women's football to know her story.

Lily played as a winger for the Dick, Kerr's Ladies and took part in the first ever recognised women's international game between England and France in London in 1920. While playing for the Dick, Kerr's Ladies she was well known for chainsmoking Woodbine cigarettes. At six feet tall, Parr played against both male and female teams and reputedly had a harder shot than any man playing at the time. Born in 1905, she was still playing football for Preston Ladies when she was 46. During her 32-year playing career, the speedy winger scored 900 goals. It was an honour indeed to follow her into the Hall of Fame.

Fourteen years on from my induction, Lily Parr and I have been joined by the old Southampton stalwart Sue Lopez; my old teammates Debbie Bampton, Karen Walker, Marieanne Spacey, Pauline Cope and Gillian Coultard; dear friend Brenda Sempare; the first ever captain of the England national team, Sheila Parker; Joan Whalley, from the Dick, Kerr's Ladies; Sylvia Gore, who scored the England national team's first ever goal; and my former captain, Faye White. What a squad of players that would make.

Chapter 10

Ups and Downs

With the limited experience of the 2001 Euros under our belt, the next task out on the pitch was to qualify for the 2003 World Cup. We were not drawn in an easy group – Germany, the Netherlands and Portugal. And after our first three games, we were playing catch up. Germany beat us 3–1 away, and we shared draws against the Netherlands at home, 1–1, and Portugal away, 0–0. The squad was still gelling, younger players like Kelly Smith and Fara Williams still settling in. But we had to buck our ideas up, and fast.

On 24 February 2002, we took on Portugal at Portsmouth's Fratton Park, in a must-win game. The players really put in a shift and rolled their sleeves up, and we ran out 3–0 winners – two for Kelly and one for Fara. There's nothing helps you settle into international football more than getting on the score-sheet. The win gave everyone a real confidence boost and, a month later, we went to the Netherlands and walloped the Dutch 4–1, with goals from Chapman, Burke, Walker and, once again, Kelly Smith.

With just Germany to play at Selhurst Park, we knew we'd won through to the qualifying play-offs as group runners-up. There's no way we could catch the Germans, but had every intention of giving them a good run for their money on English soil. The match, at Crystal Palace in May 2002, was a rip-roaring affair.

A crowd of 14,107 turned up to set a new record for an attendance at a women's game, and they saw us run the Germans close. Stefanie Gottschlich scored on 41 minutes, but we kept pressing throughout the rest of the game, and didn't look to conceding again.

But the final group table told its own story. We ended second behind Germany with eight points – two wins, two draws and two losses. Germany were top with 18 points from six wins, ten points ahead of us. They'd scored 30 goals and conceded just one. The domination of the Germans in world football was just beginning.

In the play-off semi-finals, we faced Iceland home and away. After a committed 2–2 draw in Reykjavík, we beat the Icelanders 1–0 at St Andrew's, Birmingham City's ground. Full steam ahead to a two-legged final against France – the prize for the winners a place at the 2003 World Cup finals. We played two of the best games since I'd taken over as manager. After losing by just the one goal over in France, I really felt we had it in us to overturn them at home. Despite a towering performance from the girls, we lost out 1–0 again, and France dumped us out of the World Cup at the qualifying stages.

I was bitterly disappointed. So near and yet so far. At the very least, it would mean another four years without World Cup football, and I was desperate for my players to gain experience at the highest level. It was the only way we would improve. Failing to qualify reminded me of just how steep a learning curve we were on. But my bosses at the FA continued to make it clear my appointment was not results-based. It was all about growing and developing the game and, by 2002, it was clear a lot of new initiatives were being put in place.

Life is all about ups and downs, and how you deal with them. Despite our failure to get out of the qualifiers, 2002 would unexpectedly end on a huge personal high note. One morning in October a letter arrived on the doormat containing a royal crest on the outside. I was away with England and Michelle rang me to ask if she should open it. She did and it was a letter from the Lord Chancellor informing me I had been nominated to receive an OBE. Did I accept? We were elated and really felt that this honour was not just for me, but for women's football. It was a real measure of what progress was being made in the game. We were being recognised, we were visible.

Anyone nominated is sworn to secrecy until the honours list is published officially in the *London Gazette*, so Michelle decided to hide the letter in a book until I returned home and was able to send an official reply to accept. I was so busy that, as the next few weeks flew by, replying to the letter went to the back of my mind. Then I suddenly remembered it, but Michelle had forgotten which book she'd placed the letter in. We have a lot of books in our house. Eventually, after much searching, we finally found the letter. We also discovered we only had a couple of days to the deadline to reply. Otherwise, the offer would be withdrawn.

I returned it just in time, and a couple of months later, on 10 December 2002, I was sat in a car outside the gates of Buckingham Palace with my mum, my brother Brian and Alan, waiting to be admitted into the grounds. Originally, I'd asked Michelle to be one of my three official guests, but Alan was adamant he wanted to be there. Michelle said to take Al – 'He likes all that airy fairy stuff.' So the three of them were all given security checks and then confirmed as my guests on the day. We met Michelle and Al's wife Gaynor later for a really nice lunch.

One thing you should know about Buckingham Palace is that it's bloody freezing. I remember looking around the huge rooms and endless corridors and thinking, 'Blimey, they must get some monster energy bills.' The day of the ceremony just happened to be the coldest of the year so far. You're not allowed inside the grounds until the preliminaries to the ceremony begin. But it was so cold that the Queen took pity on the 200 people outside and got them to open the gates and let us in early.

Once inside, you're separated from family and friends. An official takes the honour recipients through to another room to guide everyone through the process of what's about to happen and how. When your name is called you walk across the red carpet towards the Queen and, if you're a man, bow from the neck; if you're a woman, you curtsey. She holds out her hand for you to shake and then has a short conversation with you. So, all primed, we were taken through to meet the Queen.

She stands on a box and looks down on you. I don't think this is a status thing. She is very small and, for the taller award recipients, she needs to be at eye level and be high enough to pin the award on to everyone's chests. I'm not trying to be funny, but her voice is so high-pitched and posh, I wanted to laugh.

She was really well briefed, though. She knew who I was and said, 'So you're women's football. How did you get into that?'

I pointed over towards Alan in the audience and replied, 'Because of him.'

I know she asked me a couple more questions, and I know I must have replied but, even straight after the ceremony, I couldn't remember what we'd discussed. Everything went into a sort of blur. I'm sure a lot of other people who've received an honour at Buckingham Palace have experienced the same phenomenon. You think you're calm, cool and collected, then suddenly all of the pomp and circumstance of being there in the presence of the

Queen, in one of the most historic and famous buildings in the world, starts to have its effect. I'm not an over-emotional person, but having my mum there, who I love to bits, made me feel so proud. As mum and daughter, we'd been through so much together in our lives. Having Brian there, my brother and one of my most loved and closest friends, and Alan, my mentor and constant supporter – and thinking back to being a skinny little black kid kicking a football around on a south London housing estate – well, the emotions undoubtedly fogged my brain on the day.

Years later, in 2010, I would be honoured again, this time with a CBE, and Michelle joined me for that one. There was an Asian guy who'd won an award for services to his local community, and he completely lost it. I know it's not funny, and he must have felt mortified, but after he'd been given his medal, the poor guy got so overwhelmed he wandered around all over the chamber like he was lost, turned his back on the Queen, which you are absolutely not meant to do, and eventually had to be led back to his seat by one of the Beefeaters. From my earlier experience, I could understand how he must have been feeling, and I had every sympathy with the guy.

Receiving the OBE and CBE were both as much recognition of women's football in England as they were of my work within it. They were both proof that the game was being increasingly talked about and noticed. As, I guess, its standard-bearer, the honours have come to me. But so far as I'm concerned, they are for the game. Throughout my career, I've been extraordinarily proud to receive a number of other honours, such as honorary degrees from the Universities of Roehampton, Leeds, Nottingham, Loughborough, York, East London and St Mark and St John. These, too, I view as honours for women's football.

Chapter 11

2005

The year began with bad news for English women's football. With cruel timing, the richest club in the world, Manchester United, announced they were pulling out of women's football – just months before the Women's Euro 2005 tournament was to be staged in Manchester and the north-west. At the end of the season, their women's team would be disbanded. It shocked everyone involved in women's football. Teams that came under the umbrella of the leading men's clubs benefited hugely from improved training facilities, coaching support, better marketing and publicity, and the kudos of being part of old established clubs and their fan base. While we were trying so hard to grow the women's game, it was depressing that such a great club was saying, in as many words, that women's football didn't matter to them. The club said they wanted to focus their commitment to women's football on coaching youngsters up to the age of 16. The truth is that, by law, United were obliged to coach girls up to 16 in order to be permitted to have a boys' academy. That they made their decision at a time when Manchester was to become the shop window for women's football in England showed how little they cared.

There was, however, massive commitment at the FA to ensure that the Euros would be a success. Everyone had worked so hard on the bid to get the European Championships in England, and it was vital to show the world that this new emerging confidence around England women's football could deliver on a big stage.

It was important for me, from a credibility point of view, as well. I'd managed to get more funding to set up the structures to improve the women's game, and now some proof was needed that it had begun to bear fruit. Personally, not qualifying for the 2003 World Cup had really disappointed me. I regarded it as a lost opportunity to show just how far we'd developed at international level – but the reality was that the best teams were still in a different class. Failure to qualify also meant we missed out on vital tournament experience. So, in the build-up to the 2005 Euros, we tried to play as many back-to-back friendlies as possible, to learn how quickly the players recovered between games. In essence, we were trying to recreate the relentless nature of tournament football by playing every few days.

For 2005, we were far from favourites. England still lagged a long way behind the top sides like Germany, France and the Scandinavians. But my hope was that we could get ourselves out of the group stages and play some attractive football. For the tournament, I targeted three areas for us to focus on tactically – defending, possession and player rotation. First the focus was on our pressing line, because that's where your defending begins. We needed to understand the teams we were up against. How high you set your pressing line depends upon your opponents. In our group, for example, we had drawn two Scandinavian teams – Finland and Sweden – both of whom were different in style. For the Sweden game, we played a deeper line because of the incredible movement of their forwards, Hanna Ljungberg and Victoria Svensson. We knew they would be looking to get the ball behind our defence. So for that game, we would have a slightly deeper pressing line. The Finns were big and physical, so I wanted us to press a few yards higher up the pitch, to squeeze the amount of high balls they could launch into our final third.

So we tried to focus on defence, winning the ball and then transitioning quickly from defence into attack. When we got the ball, we needed to move it as swiftly as possible. In training, Brent and I prepared the players by organising a lot of small-sided passing and moving drills, with minimal touches, single touches. This also helped the players concentrate on keeping possession. But immediately you lose the ball, you have to transition into defence. It's easier to attack than it is to defend. So a lot of our drills reflected that, too. They were all about what happens when you lose the ball. We'd gradually begun to tighten up more defensively, which offered the opportunity to be a little more expansive. In our friendly games before the tournament, we'd found more width, pressed higher and placed much more pressure on our opponents. But friendlies aren't tournament games. Now we had to start proving ourselves in serious competitive football.

The FA had also sunk an unprecedented amount into marketing the tournament. When we arrived in Manchester as a squad ten days before the first match, the city was full of huge billboards advertising the Euros and featuring larger than life images of our players.

In consultation with the FA, Umbro had designed a new kit especially for the tournament. The shirt had a V-neck with a red cross sitting on the right shoulder and reminded me a lot of the classic American women's tops. The strip was stylish and tailored and made us look good. It was a million miles away from the baggy old men's shirts I used to wear for England. Twenty-feet tall up on the billboards, our players in their new strip looked inspiring. And, excitingly, sports shops in the middle of Manchester were actually selling replica shirts – the first time I'd ever seen that happen for the England Women's team. Our marketing person, Bev Ward, had played a blinder and managed to get us a lot of unprecedented press coverage in national newspapers and magazines. After years of trying, myself and the squad were suddenly getting major features and interviews, particularly in the broadsheets. I had never been so busy with press interviews.

Bev had also arranged for the players to go into lots of local schools, to talk about the Euros and women's football in general, which clearly made a big impact on the young girls they got to talk with, who now had female footballing role models to look up to, not just famous male players. A real buzz was starting to grow around the tournament, and particularly the England team.

We took over a suite of rooms in our Manchester hotel, which included a general office, a meeting room and an area for talking and relaxing together. Our HQ, if you like. We put together an Inspiration Wall that was full of photos of the players scoring goals, making tackles and saves, celebrating and so on – positive and inspiring features and newspaper clippings; anything that reminded the players just how far they had come as a unit.

One end of the room was full of laptops that contained video footage of our three group-stage opponents, which the players were encouraged to watch to pick out members of the opposition who may be marking them or whom they would mark, and to analyse their playing styles and the way the teams were set out. The coaching staff and I would give them more detailed information about how to play against their opponents, but it was important that the players also did their own analyses to really understand what made the opposition tick, ascertain their strengths – and their exploitable weaknesses.

We tried to look after the players as best as we could within the camp itself. For those players who had children, we booked extra rooms so they could have their families with them. Families didn't have to pay for a thing and had their meals thrown in.

It was a young squad. Our oldest player was Vicky Exley, who was only 29. Twelve of the 20-player squad were under 25. I picked Rachel Brown, Leanne Hall and Jo Fletcher as my three goalies. In defence was my captain Faye White, alongside Alex Scott, Rachel Unitt, Mary Phillip, Lindsay Johnson and Anita Asante. In midfield and up front were Fara Williams, Katie Chapman, Emily Westwood, Vicky Exley, Amanda Barr, Rachel Yankey, Casey Stoney, Karen Carney, Kelly Smith, Jody Handley and Eniola Aluko.

As host nation we had the honour of opening the tournament against Finland, the only team at the tournament below us in the world rankings. They were the least fancied nation in our group, which featured fellow Scandinavians and big hitters, Sweden and Denmark. If we stood any chance of getting out of the group, the onus was on us to beat the Finns.

All the games were played in the football hotbed of the north-west, in Manchester, Blackburn, Blackpool and Warrington. The Finland match was to be played at the new City of Manchester Stadium, and the players got some inkling of how big it was going to be when our coach was given a police escort to the ground because the roads were so busy. We arrived around an hour and a half before kick-off, and people were already streaming into the ground. We all made our way into the dressing rooms. There were a few gasps, as most of the girls had never been in a changing area so big or luxurious. As was our custom, we took the players out on to the pitch to let the kit people get on with arranging the gear. The turf was in superb condition and you could sense that the players were feeling we'd come up in the world a good few notches. Originally built for the 2002 Commonwealth Games and then converted into a football stadium for Manchester City, the stadium is a truly unique world-class sporting venue. It was designed as a continuous oval bowl with three tiers of seating at the sides and two tiers at either end, and you could sense by the way the players kept gazing with awe around the stadium that pulses were racing. We had ten minutes walking around, chatting and trying to put one another at ease, and then returned to the dressing room for pre-match talks to remind the players about our game-plan for one last time.

Then, as the players got stripped and changed and went through their own pre-match routines, I walked back out on to the pitch to grab a few quiet moments alone, to collect my thoughts. But as I walked out through the tunnel, it was anything but quiet. There were already thousands in the ground and, as they spotted me, a massive roar went up. I remember thinking, 'Oh my God, there are A LOT of people here.' I was totally taken aback by the atmosphere that was already building in the ground and went straight back into the dressing room to prepare the girls and put them in the picture about what to expect, in terms of the huge crowd. In the dressing room, generally, I always tried to be calm before a game. For the Finland game, I told the squad to just try to enjoy the occasion. I tried to take the seriousness out of the situation as much as I could, because the girls were obviously feeling a lot of pressure already. The more you experience big-match atmospheres, the more you can manage them yourself as a player. But so few of my squad had any tournament experience. Some tried to relieve the tension of waiting to go out there by getting the headphones on and listening to their favourite music. Some were busy, nervously chatting. Others were in their own world. Brent and I reminded one or two individual players about some of the personal battles they had to win against the Finns but, generally, tried to keep things light and relaxed.

When they were warming up, I got Fara to pass the ball to me, and then I'd pass it back at angles, to make her move and get her mind focused. It had become a bit of a tradition between us, and it certainly seemed to help Fara.

The opening minutes were electric, but for all the wrong reasons. It was an electricity of sheer nervous energy. I could tell from the looks on some of the players' faces that they were dazed and totally overwhelmed by the atmosphere in the ground. The experience for them was so new. The stands were a sea of red and white: St George's flags, thousands of people wearing face paint, thousands more in England shirts. As we would discover after the game, the crowd of 29,029 was not only the biggest ever to watch an England women's match, but the biggest ever in a Euros tournament. This was big-match pressure, and so many of the girls had never been in a big tournament before. Aged just 17, Karen Carney was pulling on an England shirt for only the third time.

The players were nervy and kept giving the ball away. Everything was frantic, there was no composure at all. I remember Fara Williams looked like she was on a different planet. Her mouth was permanently open, her eyes drawn to the crowd.

By comparison, the Finns looked comfortable in possession – until the 18th minute, that is. Suddenly we were handed a massive stroke of luck. The Finnish goalie Satu Kunnas made an absolute hash of a Karen Carney free-kick, spilled the ball and defender Sanna Valkonen got an agonising last touch to help it roll over the goal-line. This fortunate own goal seemed to settle the girls. Soon afterwards, Kelly Smith cracked a shot against the crossbar, and Amanda Barr was alert enough to head in the rebound and double our lead.

But after the interval, the Finns were revitalised. Minutes into the second half, Anna-Kaisa Rantanen side-footed home from the edge of the box to pull one back and make it 2–1, then the Finns piled on the pressure and, with just over a minute of normal time remaining, Laura Kalmari tapped a goal in from close range to equalise. But the crowd would not be denied a win, and they began to roar the girls on. Two minutes into injury time, Eniola Aluko played a perfectly weighted through pass into Karen Carney, who was still a Brummie schoolgirl at the time. Fifteen yards out from goal, and with total audacity, Carney calmly chipped Satu Kunnas to give us a winning start to the campaign. Two teenagers combining beautifully and, for me, that signalled the great promise of things to come from both. We were off to a winning start.

For the first time as England manager, I experienced something I would soon have to get more used to dealing with. In the aftermath of the game, Karen instantly became big sporting news. A 17-year-old kid had come on with seconds to go and scored the winning goal. The press swamped her. Everyone wanted an interview with Karen; reporters camped outside her parents' home. For a young kid she dealt with it well, but in the end I had to say, 'No more.' It was becoming a major distraction for Karen, and I had to manage the situation. I was acutely aware that it was

ad backs girls' fight to play football for school

15, have been told they cannot play for their school, even though sportsmaster Mr. Alan Moreland says they are as good if not better than the boys in the team.

Jane and Hope are pupils at Abbey Wood School, in

Eynsham Dr...
the school ar...
with the Le...
Sedge Hill S...
wanted to pr...
but Abbey...
until Hope...

...term called in to make up the num-

who are no strangers to soccer — they play regularly for the women's football team ...dis...

are not allowed to play football with boys, and if they do, they are banned from playing in W.F.A. matches.

master, to tunities Cor
And the F.A. have ruling. The girls to pla

Football aces are shown red card

WHEN Abbey Wood School football team take the field it's always without two of the best players in the school who are forbidden to play.

The two players have also represented their country, but still can't get into the team. Why? Because they are girls.

Both Hope Powell and Jane Bartley, both 17, would easily make the team, but Football Association rules do not allow mixed teams.

Girl football equal rights

Hope's on the ball

Soccer girl who gets a kick out of playing cool

Jane Ba...
football

by Mark Langlands

IT MAY be hard for fans at the Den to stomach — but Millwall's brightest hope for the future is a schoolgirl.

Hope Powell, 16, has already pulled on an England shirt in a vital women's international clash.

Her club side Millwall Lionesses are also

from page 1

to the age of 11, but after that they may not, except in friendly matches and then only when both head teachers have given permission.

Mr. Moreland told the Ken-

football, they woul...
ting the door on a career opportunity."

Both Jane and Hope are realistic about their predicament. They have stopped playing for the school, so they

Banned from playing with the boys

The 1983 Millwall squad with me second from the right on the back row

Proudly wearing my first England cap

With Samantha Britton in my early England playing days

In action for Millwall Lionesses in the early Eighties

© Eileen Langsley/Getty Images

Relaxing with my
England teammates
Brenda Sempare,
Angie Gallimore and
Linda Curl on tour
in Italy in 1984

Getting my hands
on the Women's FA
Cup with Croydon
in 1996

Niagara

THERAPY W.F.A
SEMI FINA

Matchball Spon
CLUBSCE
Continental S
TOURS

10.30 am
LEASOWE PACIFIC L.F.C
v
RANGERS L.F.C

2.30 pm
FRIENDS OF FULHAM L.F.C
v
BRONTE LADIES F.C.

WOMEN'S FO
ASSOCIATION

At LINCOLN CITY F.C., SINCIL BANK, LINCOLN

SUNDAY, MARCH 5TH, 1989

Millwall v Fulham

WOMEN'S FOOTBAL

NIAGARA THERAPY
WFA CUP FINAL

Friends of Fulham LFC

V's

Leasowe Pacific LFC

Manchester United FC
Old Trafford, Manchester

Saturday 22nd April, 1989
Kick off: 2.00 p.m.

THE WFA

F.A. WOMENS
PREMIER LEAGUE (Monday)
NATIONAL DIVISION

JOHN 311 0499
Niagara 291 5206
Jenny 853 0736

DONCASTE
BEL

CRO

A
WEL
SUNDA
K

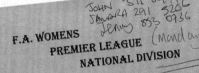

CROYDON
WOMENS
FC Founded 1991

1996/1997
FAW PREMIER LEAGUE
NATIONAL DIVISION

Programme £1

Croydon Arena
Albert Road
South Norwood
London SE25
Tel 0181 654 8555

CROYDON

A bit of women's
football history

Coming to the end of my playing career with England women in 1997
© Clive Brunskill/Getty Images

The first ever female on the Uefa B Licence course, in 1998 © Rachel Pavlou

Celebrating with Karen Carney after her winner in the 2005 Euros opener against Finland
© Alex Livesey/Getty Images

Enjoying some time off with Alan May at the 2001 Euros in Germany © Alan May

Early days in charge of England

Preparing for the 2007 World Cup in China © Paul Gilham/Getty Images

Eni Aluko shows off her silky skills against Argentina in the 2007 World Cup
© Paul Gilham/Getty Images

With my good friend Rachel Pavlou after an under-19s game against Norway in 2009 © Laurence Griffiths/Getty Images

Honoured: at Buckingham Palace to pick up my MBE in 2010 © WPA Pool/Getty Images

Making a point to the players in the World Cup qualifier against Turkey in 2010

© Matt Lewis/Getty Images

On the touchline for the 2010 World Cup qualifier against Austria © Phil Cole/Getty Images

With Kelly Smith and Rachel Yankey at the 2012 Women's Football Awards as they both receive their 100th England caps © Jan Kruger/Getty Images

David Cameron gives us a send-off from 10 Downing Street for the 2011 World Cup © Handout/Getty Images

Good luck: a handshake for my skipper Faye White before the 2011 World Cup game against New Zealand © Alex Livesey/Getty Images

Willing the players on against New Zealand © Martin Rose/Getty Images

In the tunnel before
the quarter-final
against France

Karen Bardsley applauds
the fans as England go
out of the World Cup on
penalties against France

Working for UEFA at a study visit in St Albans © Tom Dulat/Getty Images

At the launch of the Women's Super League in 2011 © Jan Kruger/Getty Images

Boys and girls come out to play: a joint training session with the GB Men's team at the 2012 London Olympics © Jamie McDonald/Getty Images

Facing the media with Stuart Pearce at a press conference for the Games

© Paul Gilham/Getty Images

Olympic jubilation! The girls celebrate scoring against Cameroon

© Julian Finney/Getty Images

On song: singing the national anthem with Keith Rees and Tracy Lewis before Great Britain v Canada © Julian Finney/Getty Images

On top of the world: celebrating with the Team GB players after their win against mighty Brazil © Julian Finney/Getty Images

Kim Little gets stuck in for Team GB against Brazil's Marta © Jamie McDonald/Getty Images

On the touchline with Brent Hills, Pippa Bennett and Naomi Datson for a friendly against Japan in 2013 © Richard Heathcote/Getty Images

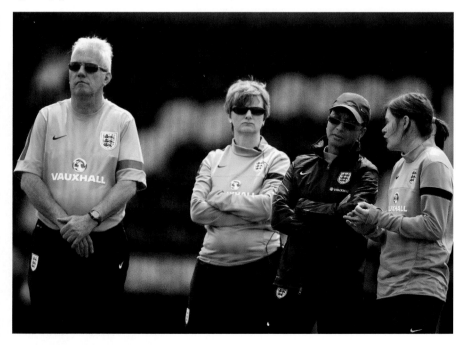

Gutted: a dejected England ponder an early exit from the 2013 Euros after defeat against France © Christof Koepsel/Getty Images

A pat on the back for Jill Scott after the Russia game at the 2013 Euros © Christof Koepsel/Getty Images

Teaching a FIFA class in The Gambia 2015

a balancing act. For years, we'd all been desperate for more coverage of the women's game in England – it was vital to us in building the profile of the sport. But, equally, I was in charge of a squad of international players at a major tournament – our first for a decade. I had to keep their feet on the ground and keep them focused on the upcoming games.

For our following match, against Denmark, we drove 25 miles up the A666 in our team coach to Ewood Park, the home of Premier League Blackburn Rovers. Though not as big or as impressive as the City of Manchester Stadium, it too had top-notch facilities and warm, welcoming club staff, who seemed genuinely overjoyed to have us playing at their ground. I was particularly taken by the club's motto which is part of its crest – '*Arte et Labore*'. Translated from the Latin, it means 'by skill and labour' – hard work. So far as I was concerned, that was a fine motto to live by.

Eni Aluko, who was only 18 at the time, had a few other things on her mind before the Denmark game even kicked off. She had one of her A levels to sit, and had spent much of the previous week with her head buried in a book, madly revising. It is credit to Eni that she was so cool about the whole thing.

We knew that a win would put us into the semi-finals. I didn't want a repeat of the big-match nervousness that had marked our start against Finland, so tried to keep the players calm before the game by having a laugh and a joke with everyone, keeping everything light. Again, we ran out in front of a good crowd – 14,695 – and though the fans made a great noise, it wasn't quite as overwhelming as the City of Manchester experience for the girls.

We started confidently but, after five minutes, my heart was in my mouth. Katie Chapman flattened Merete Pedersen in our penalty area. To be honest, from the touchline it looked like a certain pen. But the ref waved everyone away and played on. There was an audible collective sigh of relief around the entire ground.

Part of the game-plan was not to give the Danes any time on the ball, and throughout the first half the back four of Faye White, Mary Phillip, Alex Scott and Rachel Unitt did just that, constantly pressing, harrying and pushing up. Our midfield closed down superbly and tackled with real bite. On 38 minutes, Amanda Barr got a good chance but headed it wide of goal. Just before half-time we had our best chance of the match. Karen Carney picked up the ball inside in the box and slipped it through to her Birmingham City teammate Rachel Yankey. Yanks tried to curl it past the Danish goalie with the outside of her left foot, but it went agonisingly wide.

I heard one or two groans in the stand behind me. 'She should have at least got it on target.' What fans have to understand is that, at the highest level, the pace and intensity of the game literally gives players a split second to make a decision about how they're going to strike the ball and where, how they need to shape their body and what power or cushion they need to put on the shot – all while being aware of which defenders are near, who could block or thunder into them, and where the goalie is positioned. And all those decisions have to be made within nanoseconds.

Like most top sports, it's all based upon practice, practice, practice, doing the same things over and over again in training and in matches. In the pressure of the moment, out there on the pitch, with defenders flying at you and a goalie in your face, sometimes it works, sometimes it doesn't.

At half-time, I asked the girls to give me more of the same intensity and focus, and reminded them that they could be just

45 minutes away from a semi-final. In truth, they didn't really need reminding, and started the second half totally fired up. On 51 minutes, Rachel Yankey burst into the Danish area, was felled by Mariann Gajhede Knudsen and the referee pointed straight to the spot. Fara Williams was as cool as you like and rolled the ball into the bottom left corner.

For the next 20 minutes we attacked relentlessly. Williams, Exley, White and sub Eni Aluko all came close to scoring. But then it was heartbreak time. Denmark won a free-kick on the edge of our box, after a high foot by Fara Williams. Merete Pedersen stepped up and rifled a superb right-footed shot past Jo Fletcher. One each and they were back in it.

With three minutes to go, and still with one foot in the semi-finals, our defence went to sleep. The Danes won another free-kick and, totally unmarked in the box, Cathrin Sørensen headed it past Fletcher from just a few yards out. The disappointment was bitter. The Danes played out the last few minutes and the game ended 2–1. We only had ourselves to blame. After making such a great start to the second half, we gave away two needless free-kicks late on and were made to pay. Football can be a cruel game, but now we had to pick ourselves up.

My real frustration was that for the majority of the game we were the better side. Faye, who won the Player of the Match, was outstanding both as a player and a motivator, constantly cajoling and encouraging the players around her. We now went into our final group match against potentially our toughest opponents, Sweden, needing to avoid defeat against them for the first time in 21 years.

At the time, Sweden were ranked number three in the world and, two years previously, had been World Cup runners-up.

Two years before that, they had also been Euro runners-up. In Marika Domanski-Lyfors, they also had one of the best managers in women's football. I knew that I would be pitting my wits against one of the best tacticians and motivators in the business. And that my relatively young squad would be facing off against some of the best, most experienced players in the world. We were also on a run of eight straight defeats against the Swedes.

But, uncharacteristically, Sweden had not been having a good time of it in the group thus far. They could only manage draws against their Scandinavian neighbours Denmark and Finland. They came into the game needing a win to be sure of progressing. Ominously, when they had got to the finals of the World Cup and Euros, Sweden went into their final group games also needing three points, and scored vital wins on both occasions. Domanski-Lyfors and her team knew all about pressure.

The tie was back at Ewood Park and I made two changes from the Denmark game – one enforced, one a tactical move. Jo Fletcher had picked up an injury so Rachel Brown took over the goalie's shirt. Against the Swedes, I needed extra pace, so decided to replace Amanda Barr with Eni Aluko up front.

Knowing they had to win, Sweden came flying out of the traps. They immediately pressed, and on three minutes won a corner. Therese Sjögran whipped in an inswinging cross which deflected off Katie Chapman into the path of Anna Sjöström. Showing real class, she coolly back-heeled it into the net. An early blow, but we had 87 minutes to get back into the game.

Eni was outstanding and ran tirelessly at the Swedish defence. On 33 minutes her sheer pace nearly created a goal when she charged down a clearance and then looped the ball goalwards. It hung in the air and then scuffed inches wide of the far post. Just before half-time, Faye White launched a strong header at goal only for it to be deflected away against the bar by a Swedish defender. Though Sweden had got the early goal, at the interval honours were even in terms of possession and pressure, and I impressed this upon the girls. We were still in it and more than holding our own against one of the world's best sides. The game was still ours to win.

We pressured early. Kelly Smith showed all her great natural skills of anticipation by flicking a Rachel Yankey cross into the path of Karen Carney, whose shot was turned wide. From the resulting corner, Katie Chapman headed narrowly over. As we continued to come forward, Domanski-Lyfors made an astute move, bringing on Frida Östberg to add some muscle to their midfield. She was a tough, combative player and started to break up our fluid movement in the middle of the park.

It was time for a slightly more experienced head to come on, so I replaced Karen Carney with Amanda Barr up front. She did a great job of getting in the faces of the Swedish defence but, in the end, they showed all of their tournament experience by pressing us back and keeping possession. Despite matching the world's number three ranked team all the way, we just couldn't find that final touch to earn ourselves a point. The game finished England 0 Sweden 1.

Just to heap on the agony, Finland unexpectedly beat the much higher-ranked Denmark, which meant that one point would have been good enough for us to qualify. We finished bottom of the group, but only one point off second-placed qualifiers Finland. The two late goals we conceded against Denmark cost us dearly and, in the end – despite all our commitment and endeavour – we didn't have the big match nous that Sweden possessed.

It was all over far too quickly. After waiting three years from being named as hosts, we were out of the tournament within six short days. But we'd made our mark on the general public. An aggregate of over 90,000 people watched our three matches – and over eight million viewed our games on BBC2. All the national newspapers contained lengthy reports of our three group games. English women's football was starting to go places.

We'd also learnt a lot about the pressures of big-tournament football. The reason the teams at the top of the tree in women's football were always winners, finalists and semi-finalists, was because they had so much tournament experience under their belts. They knew how to close matches down because they'd been there so often.

The three things that we were going to focus on in the two-year run-up to the 2007 World Cup were: rotation, defending and pressuring. At times during the 2005 Euros our movement and approach play was far too predictable. I needed to work harder at getting the players to show more movement off the ball and help them to offer one another more choices and options on the pitch. And it was patently clear from our first major tournament in years that the top teams were pressing and in your face all the time, always prepared to win the ball back. If we were going to join the top teams, we had to hardwire that pressuring ethic into the players.

With clinical predictability, Germany went on to win the final for the fourth consecutive time, 3–1 against the eventual conquerors of Sweden, Norway. What was hugely encouraging, and said much about the profile the tournament had achieved, was that even though England weren't in the final, 21,105 fans still turned up to Ewood Park. Germany's inspirational strikers Birgit Prinz and Inka Grings both got on the score-sheet, and it was a fitting end for their manager, Tina Theune-Meyer, who, after nine years in charge, had announced her retirement.

To show what a conveyor belt of talent the Germans had developed, her successor would be Silvia Neid, who had managed the Germany under-19 team that, the year before, had won the 2004 World Championship. As a player, she represented Germany 111 times and scored 48 goals from midfield – her first was less than a minute into her international debut.

The German women's football set-up has always been a huge inspiration and influence upon me. From grassroots up they've developed one of the most effective and sustainable systems both at club and international level in the entire world of women's football. Both Tina and Silvia, and their respective coaching staffs, have also epitomised generosity itself over the years, sharing their ideas and expertise. When I think about it, that's very common in the world of women's football. People share ideas, irrespective of which team or country they represent, much more so than in the men's game. There is much more of a sense of 'mission' in trying to develop and grow the women's game around the world.

After the final, I chatted with Tina, who was very complimentary about the England team. She told me, 'You're doing the right thing. Keep doing it. Just take your time.' She's been there and seen everything, so that was a real compliment.

After the dust had settled on the 2005 Euros, my next job was to try to build upon the legacy of the tournament and get England sat at the top table internationally, with the likes of Germany, France, Norway and the USA. Grassroots and youth development was vitally important, too, and we continued to improve work on that at the FA.

But to change the culture of women's football in England and to improve its profile, we needed to start regularly getting into the knockout stages of the major tournaments. With the Euros over, we now had the task of trying to qualify for our first World Cup since 1995. The 2007 tournament would be held in China. But before I could set about planning for the qualifiers, I very much had London on my mind.

6 July 2005 was decision day for who would host the 2012 Olympics. As a Londoner born and bred, I have an intense pride in my home city and was desperate for us to win the vote. I'd been lucky enough to visit the athletes' village during the Beijing Olympics, and got a massive flavour of what a buzz it brings to a city. I wanted that for my London, for all the eyes of the world to be upon our sporting prowess and our global reputation for hosting major events. I knew, too, that if we won the vote a particularly rundown area of east London would undergo complete regeneration, with new stadia and facilities built.

On decision day, I'd travelled in from south London to Soho Square to hand out some awards to youth coaches who'd been on various FA training schemes. There was an unusual buzz and sense of anticipation around FA headquarters. Everyone had an eye on TV screens around the building throughout the morning, as the five bidding cities – London, Paris, Moscow, New York and Madrid – each gave final 45-minute presentations to IOC members before the vote began.

At 11.26 a.m. exactly the electronic ballot began. As each round of voting went by from first to second to third, New York, Madrid and Moscow were successively eliminated from the race. That left just London and Paris in a head-to-head. The press, and perhaps more importantly, the bookies, had predicted that they would run out as the final two – and that the final vote would be an absolute cliffhanger. They weren't wrong.

The ballot result was announced at 12.49 p.m. and, much to the joy of the crowds of FA staff who'd gathered around TV screens, IOC President Jacques Rogge announced that the 2012 Olympics would indeed be held in London. I'm not usually the most demonstrative person, but even I was whooping and screaming. It had been a really tight vote, 54 to 50, but that didn't matter. It had only ramped up the drama. The Olympics were coming to my home city for the first time since 1948. I was overjoyed and knew it would be an absolute landmark occasion for London. There were fabulous images on the TV of thousands of people madly celebrating in Trafalgar Square. Everyone at the FA was on a complete high.

Some work colleagues were already tipping that I would be asked to manage the GB women's football team, but I had more immediate things on my mind. I couldn't stay and celebrate for too long in central London, because I had to go home and pack. Michelle and I were staying the night at Pippa Bennett's house, and then driving up to Cambridge. I was to have an operation on my hip. As a doctor, Pippa was coming to observe the op.

The years of twisting and turning as a player had taken their toll and my hip had been deteriorating to the extent that I couldn't put off the procedure any longer. They were going into my hip to vacuum out debris that had accumulated around the bone, to see if that would ease the situation. I was only in my late thirties and the surgeon wasn't keen to give a hip replacement to someone so young. So, vacuuming it was. I had a window between the 2005 Euro tournament and starting the qualifying matches for China, so I decided to bite the bullet and have it done.

I came round from the anaesthetic to see Michelle and Pippa sitting next to my bed. Being in hospital, for both patient and loved ones, can often be like being inside a bubble. You have no idea what's happening out there in the outside world. Suddenly I noticed dozens of texts on my phone. They were from all over the world and all asked if I was OK. I thought, 'How sweet that so many people are inquiring about whether the op has gone well.' What I didn't realise was that while I had been under, the centre of London had been rocked by what we now know were the 7/7 bombings. I innocently turned on the TV and, of course, learnt the awful truth. I was panic-stricken and immediately called members of my family and close friends. Michelle tried to call staff at the sandwich shop, but it was constantly engaged. My brother Brian worked in the City, but thank God he was OK, as was everyone else I knew. Others, of course, were not so lucky.

As I continued to watch the TV news film of the first survivors emerging shell-shocked into the daylight, their faces black with smoke and soot, it began to dawn that life in my home city would never be the same again. As the full horror of the casualties began to unfold, it struck me that this despicable act must have been deliberately planned to coincide with the Olympics announcement. The day before, London had been a city in celebration. A day later, the terrorists had stolen away any sense of jubilation and replaced it with an atmosphere of fear and revulsion. It was the most terrible reminder that life can be so random. Whatever your great plans and hopes and dreams, fate can step in in the most awful of ways. A friend at the FA missed a Piccadilly Line service from King's Cross by two minutes – the train that was blown up.

When I was driven home the following day, I was obviously on crutches. When I got out of the car, with some difficulty, my neighbours came out on to the street, saying, 'Oh my God, are you all right?' As soon as they saw me on crutches, they'd assumed I must have been involved in the bombings. I was happy to put their minds at rest – it was just a common or garden hip operation.

I remember the next couple of weeks around south London being incredibly tense. Not surprisingly, everyone was scared and suspicious. The bombings were all anyone could talk about, it was the only topic of conversation. The area around Hackney Road where we had our sandwich shop was home to one of the largest Muslim communities in Britain and contained a number of mosques. Tensions ran very high. There were a lot of bricks thrown and fighting going on. The police had to virtually guard some of the mosques, and particularly on Friday nights when local youths had had a few. The Far Right parties did their best to stir things up and for a good long while, the atmosphere was toxic. One day, someone spotted what they thought was a suspicious looking package near our shop. The whole row of stores was evacuated and put on lockdown. A day or two later, there was an incident on the street in which we live and the police arrived in force and sealed the entire area off. It was a scary time. Everybody became suspicious of everyone else.

Whatever the horrors of 7/7, there was one thing that the terrorists couldn't take away from the people of the city. London had the Olympics. And I had every hope that the build-up to this would focus everyone's minds on what can be so good, positive and wonderful about my home city. If the terrorists had hoped to wreck the hopes and dreams of Londoners by attacking the day after the Olympic decision, they got it all wrong.

Chapter 12
China, 2007

It was China, take two. The World Cup should have been played there four years earlier, but had to be switched to the USA at the last moment because of a serious SARS outbreak. It was no surprise that America had been chosen as back-up, given the marvellous success of the 1999 tournament and, once again, they had delivered. But, once again, without England. In 2003, of course, we had failed to qualify, so this was our first time back in a World Cup tournament since 1995 in Sweden. That had been our debut in a World Cup tournament. So we didn't exactly go to China with much experience on the world stage.

What is it about Germany? For both the England men's and women's teams, they always seem to be lying in wait for us in major tournaments. The 2007 World Cup would prove to be no exception. When the draw was made for the group stage, we came out of the hat with Japan, Argentina and, almost inevitably, the Germans.

That we had made it through to China said much about the progress we had made. After 12 years in the World Cup wilderness, we'd qualified strongly in what was a tough group that included France and the Netherlands. Six wins, two draws and no losses. We scored 29 goals at an average of over three a game – and chalked up our record store at international level: a 13–0 thrashing of Hungary in front of a hundred fans that included a first international hat-trick for Kelly Smith. We had been two up inside five minutes – 7–0 at half-time – against what was in all truth a pretty inept Hungary side. The really pleasing aspect of the game was the ruthless nature of my players. Thirteen up, but they were still pressing for more goals in injury time. In the eight qualifiers we conceded just two goals. It felt like all the hard work we had done on tightening up as a defensive unit was finally starting to pay off.

Our two most impressive performances had come in the two drawn games, both against France, 0–0 and 1–1 respectively. The latter, played in Rennes in front of 19,674, was a battle royal. I'd never seen the players so pumped up for a game. As they marched out on to the pitch, there were clenched fists and shouts of 'C'mon!' They looked so ready for the game it was untrue. The match was shown live on BBC3, and the players did the TV audience proud. We were all high-energy, pressing and pressuring, forcing the French into mistakes. We went in 0–0 at half-time, feeling confident we could press on and win the game. And, after 60 minutes, we took the lead. Fara Williams powered a header towards the French goal and it deflected in off Hoda Lattaf. In our seven previous encounters with France, we had not managed a single goal.

This seemed to wake up the opposition and they came at us in waves. Eventually, their pressure paid off and, on 88 minutes, French substitute Ludivine Diguelman scored the equaliser. It was a sickener, so late on. But we held out for the draw and that was more than good enough. At the time, the French were indisputably one of the world's best sides, and we were still wannabes. But thanks to their unexpected early 1–0 loss in the group to the

Netherlands, we were home and dry as champions and automatic qualifiers.

I knew that China would be quite a culture shock for many of the girls, so, in the January of 2007, I lobbied for us to be entered into the China Cup alongside the hosts, Germany and the USA. For the record, we lost 2–0 to China but managed two very creditable draws to the might of Germany and the USA. It was all useful preparation for the World Cup in September, as was the players' experience of conditions out there – and the food, which is very different from the dishes served in Chinese restaurants over here. They made much use of gizzards, offal and animals' bits and pieces. Most of the girls lived on rice, cereal and bread in the week or so we were out there. It was a valuable orientation experience that told us a lot about the best way to approach our preparation for the World Cup tournament.

Come September, we arrived in good shape. As a squad, we were far fitter and stronger. Thanks to Pippa Bennett, Dawn Scott and their team, our diet, nutrition and conditioning regimes were vastly improved. Though our squad may not have had the depth of a USA or a Germany, we had a very strong group of players – possibly our strongest ever – who had played together for a good few years and knew one another's games.

Arsenal had just won the UEFA Cup final and eight of their players formed the nucleus of our squad. So they were already on a high. In fact, throughout the 2000s each of my squads had at least six or seven Arsenal players in them, which I'm sure was good for the team. Their long-time boss, Vic Akers, was a great manager who taught his players a lot of good habits.

We had prepared meticulously. I personally made a number of further trips to China prior to the World Cup finals, to recce everything, from training facilities to what the local neighbourhoods were like. I got the hotels I wanted – and I got Idris. When you're playing abroad in tournaments, food is such an important part of the mix for so many reasons. Apart from the dietary and nutrition side of things, food can be an incredible comfort to athletes, something to look forward to and enjoy. As I say, the players hadn't taken to the local cuisine when we'd visited in January, and I didn't want them to suddenly have to change their diets to food they were not used to. So we were joined on the trip by our own chef, Idris. He was a marvel.

Given the minimal help he had to prepare our food and the limited use of the hotel kitchens, what he made for us was a sensation. We sent him out a couple of weeks in advance, and he hit the ground running, sourcing fresh ingredients from local markets and shops, making sure they were up to the standard he wanted. He undoubtedly helped us to do well at the World Cup.

The rest of the core team in China consisted of my two assistant coaches, Brent and Keith, Pippa Bennett, administrator Graeme, two physios Tracy Lewis and Caryl Becker, kit manager Tom, FA press officer Alex, security Yvonne, and our administrator, Caroline.

For me, preparation is everything, and another key member of the team was our full-time video analyst, Phil Worrall. His job was to research our opposition and collect data that would give me a good idea of where most of their goals came from, who their most important players were and the nature of their favoured formations, and so on. We would also regularly send DVDs to our players with clips of their own performances, so that they could study them in fine detail. Were there any little tweaks they could make to improve their own game? Were they crossing from too deep? Did they sometimes hold on to the ball for too long? I would also give the players questionnaires in which they would rate their performances, highlight areas that they had been successful in and those that disappointed them.

I know that some of the players jokingly referred to it as 'homework'. But it really made them focus on the nuts and bolts of their game. The idea was very much that they should own and take responsibility for their future improvement as players. I wanted to know that they were thinking about their own games, rather than just being told what to do.

Phil taught me how to cut and edit my own material too, because sometimes I just wanted to view the videos by myself – usually in our meeting room, until the wee small hours. I never got much sleep during tournaments, and I would watch the games over and over again. What I fast realised was that the better prepared we were in terms of our knowledge of the opposition, the better we did on the pitch. Key was my scouting team, which in China included Alan, Mo, Lois Fidler, Ronald Thompson, Colin Norman and Margaret McGough. While the rest of us were concentrating on preparation for the next game, they were out around the country in pairs scouting our future opponents and putting together detailed reports for me.

When I think about what we had as a back-up team in 1995 in the World Cup in Finland, we really had travelled light years in terms of our professionalism. Back in '95, we didn't even have our own dedicated meeting room in the hotel, or our own coach to take us to training or to the stadiums.

Prior to the tournament starting, I was given an accolade that meant a great deal to me. It had become traditional that before each World Cup an All Stars team would play the host nation in an exhibition game. Rachel Brown was chosen to play in goal, and other top stars in the side included Brazil's Marta, the USA's Kristine Lilly and Cheryl Salisbury from Australia. The team was to be led by Tina Theune-Meyer, the former coach of the reigning world champions Germany, and me! FIFA asked if I would prepare the All Stars with Tina, and I felt extraordinarily honoured. She was happy for me to be joint coach. But I have so much respect for Tina, I demoted myself to be her assistant. She is a legend in women's football. Tina was the first woman in Germany to acquire a coaching licence, and as assistant manager and then manager of Germany won six European Championships, two bronze medals in the Olympics and the 2003 World Cup.

The only disagreement we had was over who should be captain. Tina wanted the hugely talented Kristine Lilly, while I thought the Cheryl Salisbury should be skipper. I liked the way she motivated the players around her and argued my case accordingly. I was so impressed with Tina. She listened to what I had to say, weighed it all up and though she was by far 'the boss' in our relationship thanks to her stellar reputation, Tina agreed that Cheryl should get the captain's armband.

This is what I loved – and aspired to – about the top managers and coaches in the women's game. The very best like Tina looked to make the best decisions, based not on ego and needing to be seen as 'right', but on what will work most effectively for the team. Tina, and her successor, Silvia Neid, are two major reasons why the German national side have been the most successful in women's world football. For me, having a winning mentality is all about having a singular vision, but listening to other opinions and taking them on board.

The FIFA Women's World Stars played China at the Wuhan Sports Centre Stadium, one of the five venues that would be used for the World Cup itself. With a population of ten million, Wuhan is central China's biggest city. Known as the 'Chicago of China', it's a dizzyingly busy transportation hub, with dozens upon dozens of expressways, roads and rail lines linking it to cities all over the country. What I found fascinating was that this stellar bunch of players, who had hundreds of caps between them, were so nervous before the game. It was so nice because they were really humble. That whetted my appetite even more for the World Cup proper. I was under no illusions. This would be the biggest deal of my life as a football manager. Did I feel nervous? I couldn't afford to be.

It was a strong squad, a lot of whom had gained valuable tournament experience together in the 2005 Euros. I had tried to forge a mix of youth and experience: Lianne Sanderson was just 19, Jill Scott, Carly Telford, Karen Carney and Eni Aluko, 20-year-olds; Vicky Exley, at 31, and the hugely experienced Mary Phillip, 30, were the senior heads in the squad. Alongside them, I picked Rachel Brown, Alex Scott, Casey Stoney, Katie Chapman, Fara Williams, Kelly Smith, Rachel Yankey, Anita Asante, Siobhan Chamberlain, Rachel Unitt, Sue Smith, Jody Handley, Lindsay Johnson and my captain, Faye White. Apart from Doncaster Belle Vicky Exley, and Sue Smith and Carly Telford from Leeds United, the rest of the 20 all played for just three teams – Arsenal, Chelsea and Everton – which meant there were a lot of girls used to playing with one another, week in, week out.

The experts I consulted told me that generally most people recover from jet lag at a rate of one day for each eastward time zone travelled. So with that in mind we flew out to China eight days before we were due to play our first game against Japan, in Shanghai's Hongkou Stadium, the 32,000-seater ground of Chinese Premier side Shanghai Shenhua FC.

For the players and staff, Shanghai was an eye-opener. It's China's largest city by population – bigger even than the capital Beijing – and home to the world's biggest container port. Everything in Shanghai is on a large scale, even its spectacular skyline. We had our own coach and dedicated drivers, but just getting the couple of miles from the hotel to the ground was a major undertaking. The traffic seemed to be in permanent gridlock, day and night. We had to set off an hour early just to ensure we got to the ground on time. And when the traffic did move, the driving was crazy. The cars and lorries were pretty unpredictable, but worse were the millions of motorbikes and scooters. They didn't need driver's licences and seldom seemed to follow any kind of traffic rules, weaving perilously around all over the road, between the trucks and taxis. They certainly didn't worry too much about pedestrians, who just seemed to be moving obstacles to be driven around. Or not, as the case may be. Watching the mayhem from our windows, we were all phenomenally grateful to be on a coach.

Our opening fixture represented a tall order for us. They were a good Japanese side, ranked eighth in the world at the time, with plenty of tournament experience. Apart from my old teammate Mary Phillip, none of my players had ever played in a World Cup before. We went into the game as underdogs.

My preparation for the Japan game proved to be the most complicated and intensive I'd ever undertaken, before – or since. I had sent Mo to scout them at a friendly before the World Cup. She came back in awed confusion, none the wiser as to how they managed to play their system. They constantly interchanged roles, played in acute triangles, overlapped. Their movement and execution was fantastic. So I had to sit down for hours and hours watching endless video footage of how they played. I had to come up with a game-plan to play against them – and it was bloody hard work.

I focused on trying to defend their movement, understanding how they linked up and how we could penetrate their thirds. Going forward, I wanted the players to exploit their full-backs and get numbers up quickly to support in the final third.

As it was, the match turned out to be an absolute roller coaster of delight and disappointment. The first half was goalless but not without incident. Eni Aluko and Kelly Smith came close a number of times and, as the half went on, we started to rack up the corners and possession around their box. It was to be in the second half when the real drama began to unfold. In the 55th minute, Katie Chapman was penalised for a foul on Homare Sawa just on the edge of the box. Aya Miyama sent in a curling shot past Brown and Japan were ahead.

The players showed what character they had by continuing to attack with real intent and, in two short minutes, Kelly Smith showed her class by turning the game on its head. With ten minutes to go, Carney found Smith in space in the area, Kelly turned and steered a left-foot shot past the Japanese keeper for the equaliser.

What happened next led to me giving Kelly a real telling off. She raced off down the touchline in her goal celebration, then stopped, slipped off her boot and kissed it in front of the Japanese bench. I could absolutely appreciate her joy – she'd scored at the World Cup after coming back from a catalogue of horrendous injuries – but her goal celebration looked arrogant and disrespectful, almost as though it was calculated to rile the Japanese players. Having had so many injuries, I didn't want for her to suddenly become a target for any rough stuff or revenge. So I told her, 'Never again, thank you very much.'

A minute after she'd pulled her shoe back on, Kelly burst into the area again and shot. The goalie could only parry it back into her path, and Kelly scored from the rebound. I was utterly elated. This could be the winning start to the campaign that we'd all dreamt about. After over three minutes of added time we looked to be safe, home and dry. And then the fates – and the ref – stepped in.

Mary Phillip was very harshly penalised for an innocuous looking challenge on one of their attackers. From the resulting free-kick, Miyama rifled home again to score the equaliser. A second after the ball hit the back of the net, the ref blew for full time. It was a cruel way to lose the three points and I was so frustrated for the girls.

But there were so many positives to draw from the game. Number one: the fact we had scored two goals in the last ten minutes showed how fit and strong we now were. Second, it was clear that, at the highest level, Kelly Smith was indeed a world-class player. And thirdly, after a good, inspiring performance, we looked confident and ready for anyone. The players had stuck to the game-plan against an unusually talented side, and got through it with credit.

And then it was Germany. In 2007, they were ranked number one in the world. They came to Beijing as reigning world champions and, of course, had already won the European Championships six times. Their team captain and all-time top scorer, Birgit Prinz, had just passed 200 caps. She led a hugely experienced squad full of world-class players, which included goalie Silke Rottenberg, who in 126 games had kept a clean sheet on no fewer than 67 occasions. To say they were formidable would be an understatement. Add to that the simple fact that we had never beaten Germany and you get some idea of the task ahead.

I'd never seen my players so nervous before a game. A couple of them were physically sick in the dressing-room toilets, and there was an unusual silence, a lack of the customary banter. I did everything I could to lighten the situation and told them, nay promised them, 'Today will be a good day.' I don't think anyone believed me. But I really felt that if we executed the game-plan, we would get rewarded.

And then I talked strategy. This is the part of the game I love the most. Pitting your wits against the best. My assistants weren't sure about my plan at all, but I told them to trust me. I knew it would work. The plan was to try to stifle the Germans: high intensity right across the pitch, break up play, everyone making themselves available to defend. Put Faye White on Birgit Prinz and try to cut off the supply lines to their forward players. We couldn't allow Germany to play their natural game.

In the first few minutes, our nerves were settled. Kelly chased down a high ball and fired home a shot that went narrowly past the right-hand post. It wasn't a goal but it had left the German defence struggling and buoyed our players. From then on, we fought for our lives and showed resilience that I think shocked the Germans. It was really tough out there. For long spells, they kept piling forward in numbers. But my players stuck together, threw in tackles and kept their collective nerve.

I brought Rachel Yankey on from the bench. Though she would I'm sure admit she was never the greatest when it came to defending, Yanks made a stupendous block. In that moment, she exemplified the all for one and one for all spirit of the team.

It was a lung-bursting game. But our improved strength and fitness saw us get over the wire with a 0–0 draw. Faye White was inspirational and marked Birgit Prinz out of the game, deservedly winning player of the match. But, really, the entire team put in big-game performances. I gazed across at the German manager Silvia Neid, and I could tell from the look on her face that 0–0, for them, was like a loss. Our strategy had worked and my players had executed the plan to perfection. It reminded me of the 1–1 we had played against France in the qualifiers, when we had also played with such intensity and focus, and remained concentrated right to the final whistle.

In terms of getting past the group stage and into the quarter-finals, everything was still alive. The last game was against Argentina, who had lost their opening fixture in the group 11–0 to Germany. But I was under no illusions about what a tough task they would present. They only arrived two days before the tournament started and had had little time to orientate themselves for the Germany game. Argentina would be stronger and in a better shape for our game with them. They'd lost narrowly to Japan, 1–0, and we had to beat them to be sure of progressing.

Our first two games were intense affairs, and I worried how much that might have taken out of my players. This was where all the preparation came into play. Tournament football is so different from one-off games. The matches come thick and fast every few days, and the top teams all possess tournament savvy. Did we?

I needn't have worried so much. Like they had in their drubbing against Germany, Argentina managed to implode in spectacular fashion. After just eight minutes, and with no England player remotely near her, Eva González planted a stunning header into the top corner of her own net, and the floodgates opened. A minute later, Jill Scott scored her first international goal, and then in the second half they gifted us two penalties – both converted by Fara Williams and sub Vicky Exley respectively – and once again Kelly Smith scored a brace. The 6–1 scoreline didn't flatter us, and we were improving as the tournament progressed. We were in the quarter-finals.

Now it was just the small matter of playing the USA, the number-two ranked team in the world, for a place in the semi-finals. And much to my disappointment, it would be without Fara. She had picked up another yellow against Argentina and would miss the game. This was a big blow for us. The USA midfield was full of flair and Fara's strength and tackling power would be much missed.

We moved north to Tianjin, a coastal city, the fourth largest in China. Like Shanghai, it was hot and humid, but everyone had grown more used to the climate. And also like Shanghai, it was a city that seemed to be in a permanent state of traffic jam.

To get to Tianjin, we took an internal flight, and soon attracted a lot of attention from the native Chinese on the plane. At the time I had dreadlocks, and they were fascinated with my hair. Rachel Yankey was sat next to an old Chinese woman who must have been about a hundred years old. She started to gently stroke Rachel's face and hair, and pretty much didn't stop during the one-hour flight. Yanks was really sweet and just let her get on with it. As we were coming in to land, the old lady turned her attentions to me. She spoke with her eyes and I knew she was asking if she could stroke my dreadlocks too. But I had to make my excuses, because we were about to land and I had work to do.

The first job in hand was to get everyone into the hotel and set up our HQ, so that I could start going through videos with Phil, scouting reports from Alan and the team and start planning in earnest for the quarter-final. What a task it would be.

The USA had experience to burn. Before the World Cup had begun, their inspirational captain Kristine Lilly had already won a mind-blowing 338 international caps and scored 128 goals and, although 36 years old, she was still unbelievably fit and athletic. After China, she would play on for the USA for another three years. Their striker Abby Wambach had scored a phenomenal 85 goals in 103 matches and, among their first-choice defenders, Christie Rampone had 175 caps, Kate Markgraf 168, and Cat Whitehill 121. Their 18 outfield players had scored over 300 international goals between them. My outfield players for the tournament had scored 104 in an England shirt. Like Germany, the USA team was a machine.

I was so proud of how my players performed. It was a goalless first half and we kept the USA very quiet, while creating quite a few chances for ourselves. During the early stages, we passed the ball around confidently and Faye White, particularly, showed just what guts and determination we now had in the squad. Near the end of the first half, American striker Abby Wambach caught Faye in the face with an elbow and broke her nose. Our captain got some treatment, picked herself up and carried on playing.

In the second half, the USA showed why they were ranked number two in the world. Although we created more openings and matched them with some attractive passing football, they were ruthlessly clinical in front of goal. A second-half goal blitz saw them score three in 12 minutes and effectively end our World Cup hopes. I think 3–0 was harsh on the girls, all of whom I really felt for, particularly Rachel Brown. Their third goal was a gift from her, poor thing. She came out of goal to collect the ball and completely missed it. We were playing under floodlights at the time. She lost sight of the ball as it changed flight in the air.

In the closing stages of the game we really tried to put the Americans on the back foot. One thing's for sure, whenever you play the USA: whatever they do it's all about winning, even if it's tiddlywinks. This was the type of mentality I wanted our players to develop. Whoever came up with that phrase 'it's all about taking part' wants shooting.

I so wish we could have got further because we'd improved as we'd gone along, things were really bedding in. The players were gaining more and more big-match experience, and our performances had pushed us into the top ten of the FIFA World Rankings for the first time ever, moving up two places into tenth. Deservedly, four-goal Kelly Smith was named in the FIFA All Star Team, cementing her place among the world's elite.

Once again, Germany were clinical in beating Marta's Brazil 2–0 in the final. England finished ranked seventh. Our 0–0 draw against Germany looked even better when you consider they set a new tournament record by taking the world title without conceding a single goal in six matches. We were the only country to take a point off them. We became the first England team since my playing days in 1995 to get as far as the World Cup quarter-finals. I left China ready to prepare for the European Championship qualifiers knowing we were making good progress as a squad. Now we wanted a podium finish.

The players and most of the staff flew home, but I had other work to do in China. After each World Cup, FIFA hold a symposium for representatives from each of the participating countries. It's basically a post-mortem of the tournament – what worked well, what could be improved – and it's a great opportunity to talk football issues with women's team managers from around the world.

Michelle flew out and I got the rare treat of being a tourist for a couple of days too. We visited the Great Wall of China and became fascinated by the structure. I didn't realise that the steps were all deliberately uneven and carved at odd levels, to hinder any invading enemies. I was so tired from the nervous energy I'd expended during the World Cup that the altitude really got to me.

As I returned to England and my desk at the FA, exciting behind-the-scenes developments began to take up more of my time. Work was starting in earnest on a major new development backed by the FA, the Women's Super League. The intention was to give women's club football in England a major new re-launch: more exposure, more sponsors and increased financial backing. I was a massive supporter of this. But to get it right required a huge amount of work for everyone involved. There was the logistical side, the legal and the marketing. Anything to do with the technical side came to me. There was much to consider. How big should the Super League be? Twelve clubs had been suggested, but I argued for eight. I felt that a smaller number would make it a truly competitive league, with a real strength in depth to all of the participating clubs. How long should the season be? And how would it fit into the international calendar? How many players should be paid at each club, and how much?

I was a big advocate for it being a summer league for a number of reasons. Firstly, we wouldn't be competing against the men's season and that would hopefully allow us to build attendances among football fans, not only attracting hardcore women's football supporters, but perhaps pulling in fans new to the women's game who felt starved of footie through the summer months. And, secondly, women's football is a very technical game – playing in fine weather, when the pitches are in good condition, would show it off at its best. And, again, there were the fans who were maybe trying something new to think about, who wouldn't be put off by sitting in the freezing rain. I so remembered sloshing around on mud, ice and snow so often during my playing career, and just felt that the summer conditions would benefit the women's game the best.

The FA deserve a great deal of credit for backing the Women's Super League. It was planned to launch in 2010. That didn't happen – there were some major hiccups along the way (more of that later) – but when it did eventually get off the ground, the WSL was undoubtedly a massively positive way forward for women's football in England.

The year 2008 ended with a gesture from the FA that was little reported but did bring a sense of redemption to the women's game. They made an official apology for banning women from playing on FA grounds for the 50 years following 1921. I can honestly say that I was not involved in any of the thinking or decisions behind making that happen, but I welcomed it, if only as a symbolic act. For a lot of women involved in the sport through history, it's hard to forgive the FA for the damage they caused to football in this country. But we must all move on, and it was a sign of the times that the powers that be felt it necessary to acknowledge this and commit to future progress within the women's game. Women's football in England in 2008 was still far from operating in an ideal world, but step by step, things were improving; 2009 would move us on even further.

Chapter 13

Big Steps Forward

China had been a monumental experience for everybody. But international football is a conveyor belt of one tournament after another. Next up: qualification for the 2009 Euros in Finland. We were drawn in Group 1 with Spain and the Czech Republic, both of whom we expected to be our main rivals, Northern Ireland and Belarus. Strangely, the qualifiers had been timetabled so that we played our first game against Northern Ireland on 13 May 2007 – weeks before we went to the World Cup in Beijing. After a sluggish start, we won 4–0, with strikes from Kelly Smith, Katie Chapman and Lianne Sanderson, plus an Irish own goal. Our first match after China was on 27 October 2007, against Belarus in front of 8,600 fans at Walsall's Bescot Stadium. Two up at half-time through Kelly Smith and Alex Scott, we cruised to a 4–0 win with a goal just after the break from Eni Aluko and a second for Alex Scott. Then came Spain, the team I regarded as our most serious rivals. We stayed in control throughout and, oddly, the Spanish offered little threat. A second-half Karen Carney goal was enough to give us three points and go top of the group, two points ahead of the Czech Republic.

A busy March 2008, saw us beat Northern Ireland 2–0 in Lurgan and then disappointingly drop points in a dull 0–0 draw against the Czechs at Doncaster's Keepmoat Stadium. Big wins followed – 6–1 away in Belarus in May and then, crucially, a massive 5–1 victory in Prague on 28 September 2008.

The Czech encounter turned out to be a bizarre game. We were unbelievably poor in the first half and went in at half-time deservedly 1–0 down. Really rare for me, I just lost it with the players. I was so angry with their sloppiness and lack of spark, I couldn't help myself but lay into them. I told them my mum could have played better than they had in the first half. I said they'd better pull their fingers out of their arses, start sticking to the game-plan, or we could kiss goodbye to the Finland Euro finals. I'd made it clear to the girls that the Czechs would sit quite deep. We were the better team in every sense and expected to win. So it was up to us to draw them out, to limit touches, pass the ball quickly and crisply, but be patient. When they tried to come at us on the break, we needed to win the ball back quickly and be direct in getting the ball back into their final third. In the first half, my players did the opposite – they took too long on the ball and played ponderously in front of their defence. I sent them out early for the second half, so they were just kicking their heels waiting for the Czechs to come out. The girls got back to the game-plan and turned in a much more impressive performance. Kelly Smith scored a brace, followed by goals for Carney, Scott and Westwood.

Four short days later, we played the qualifying group decider against Spain in Zamora, a beautiful historic little city close to the Portuguese border. We only needed a point to remain top and qualify for Finland as Group 1 winners, but there was no way I was going there to play for a draw. Spain needed a clear two-goal victory to overturn us at the top. When it's that kind of an ask, you really need a nerve-settling early goal. Spain got the nerve-settling early goal. And then got their second just before half-time. I couldn't quite believe what I was seeing. We hadn't played at all badly, and Spain were on the back foot for most of the half. It just felt like one of those nights when the gods were against us. I started to think about what I was going to say at half-time and, bizarrely, my mind began to wander. 'If we don't qualify,' I thought to myself, 'I'll get my first summer off in bloody years.' I began to fantasise about maybe going on a safari or a cruise. And then, as the players came off, I snapped out of it. They all looked sick and grey. I think someone actually said, 'We're going out.' Unlike half-time during the Prague game, I was totally calm. I told them just to stick to the game-plan. 'It's not a problem. We're going to be all right. We're going to get something out of this game.'

It was the oddest of feelings. I knew that the girls would go out and turn things around. I was 100 per cent sure. Whether the total confidence I was exuding had any effect on the team, I'll never know. But the girls went out there in the second half and put in a fighting, battling shift. On 55 minutes, Karen Carney pulled one back. Then 13 minutes from time Kelly Smith executed a superb drag back and shot. It was 2–2 and we were through to Finland 2009 as group winners.

On form, and on a high, we flew out to the invitational Cyprus Cup tournament. An annual affair, the competition had been created as an alternative to the Algarve Cup for Women, which had been held in Portugal every year since 1994. The Algarve tournament is one of the most prestigious and longest running women's international football events. England appeared in it twice, in 2002 and 2005. It's a great competition, but was quite exclusive. They were only interested in involving the best international countries around the world. But, for me, this wasn't what England needed or what I felt was important about developing women's football in other nations. So we started going to the Cyprus Cup every year instead.

The tournament was the brainchild of former Swedish footballer Anna Signeul, who became coach of the Scotland Women's team in 2005. She was the real inspiration behind creating an annual event that would help international teams from up and down the world rankings get tournament experience. Ourselves and the Dutch totally bought into her idea and, with Anna, became co-organisers of the Cyprus Cup.

The 2009 tournament saw us teamed up against France, Scotland and South Africa in group A, while group B had Canada battling it out with Russia, New Zealand and the Netherlands. It was a great competition to be in because it gave our players much needed tournament experience on a regular, yearly basis, with three or four games played back to back over the period of a fortnight. In 2009 it also meant valuable time together as a squad in March, which was great preparation for the Euro finals later in the summer.

Our first game saw us cruise past a developing South Africa side 6–0, with three first-half goals from Williams, Sanderson and Smith, then one from Steph Houghton and a brace from Chapman in the second. We fought a creditable 2–2 draw with France, twice coming back from behind with goals from Carney and Stoney, before sealing the group with a 3–0 victory over Scotland – Aluko, Emily Westwood and Jessica Clarke all on the mark. Canada won group B, so we would face them in the final in Nicosia. We got off to a poor start, conceding to a Christine Sinclair goal in the 14th minute, after a defensive mix up. But the girls bounced back with three goals before half-time from Sanderson, Smith and Williams.

We played a mature second half, not allowing the Canadians to threaten. But for the brilliance of their keeper, Karina LeBlanc, the 3–1 margin of the win would have been much wider. We'd won the Cyprus Cup and all was looking good for Finland.

But before the Euros came along there was much rejoicing at the FA. Finally, the long fought for central contracts programme was brought in. My team and I had spent a long time trying to, first of all, get the FA board to agree to the idea of central contracts, then work with them and the Professional Footballers' Association to ensure that the contracts were right for the players. I was desperate to get this implemented, not simply because Rachel Pav (the FA women's development manager) kept badgering me to do it, and I wanted to get her out of my ear! But, more seriously, there was a sense we were asking the players to be more professional but still treating them like amateurs. They had daily personal training programmes that our fitness team put together, and they had to fit these in alongside full-time jobs. Casey Stoney, for example, was having to get up at 5 a.m. every day to fit in her training programme before going to work. I looked at how they operated central contracts systems in hockey, cricket and a number of other sports, both men's and women's. I did a lot of research into how they were put together and which ones seemed to work the best. Basically, I wrote the first draft of the document and then passed it on to the FA's lawyer, Mary Guest, who tidied it up.

But 2009 had also brought unexpected new pressures to the potential deal. The banking crisis and the global recession were beginning to take their toll in the UK. As a consequence of this new financial climate, the FA had decided to defer the launch of the Women's Super League until 2011. They were concerned about potential sponsorships, their own investment and that, broadly, a global financial meltdown was probably not the best time to launch such an ambitious new venture.

The FA's decision to postpone the launch of the WSL caused a lot of annoyance in women's sport. The Women's Sport and Fitness Foundation chief executive, Sue Tibballs, went so far as to say, 'If anybody wanted a clear indication of the FA's regard for women's football this is it. They were looking at their budgets to see what they could cut and women's football was an easy option.'

I was disappointed that the WSL would have to wait a little longer, as I believed that a stronger elite league could only help the development of women's football and gain it more ongoing coverage and exposure. With that would come more sponsorship and marketing opportunities and more money would come into the women's game. But, on the upside, I was delighted that the FA board agreed to go ahead with the new central contracts deal, despite what was happening in the wider world, economically speaking. You can't put everything on hold, and it was so important for the women's game that this was put in place.

The FA guaranteed a central contracts deal that would initially involve 20 players. Effectively, it allowed footballers to go part-time with their day jobs to focus further on their development in the sport. They were allowed to work up to 24 hours a week to help boost their income. It meant that I could have my players more available and they could concentrate more on training and playing. Just as importantly, they could get adequate rest and recovery time in between, without the pressures of having to work 35-plus hours a week.

Much was made at the time about what the central contracts would pay – £16,000 per player per year – and what a drop in the ocean it was compared to what men earned in the Premier League.

At the time, most made double that per week. But, as ever, it was an unfair comparison with the men's game. Yes, I would have loved the players to have been paid more than £16,000, but the reality is there's no comparison between the economic power of the men's game and the kind of money that's in women's football.

Some of the players weren't happy that everyone was being paid the same, and argued that the older, more experienced players should get more than the younger ones. However, it was a start. This was a major step forward for us in the mission to compete at the very top level in the world.

There was an exciting new development in the level beneath the senior squad in 2009 too. The future looked even better when Mo Marley took a very talented under-19 squad to the European Championships in Belarus in July. Mo is one of those people who you just want everything good to happen for. She was a really good, committed player and had, latterly, taken to coaching like a duck to water. The young players had so much time and respect for her wisdom and great sense of humour, and that showed in the squad she brought to Belarus – there was a great togetherness and a great sense of confidence. Thrillingly, they got to the final and played Sweden at the Haradski Stadium. Everton Ladies striker Toni Duggan scored the opening goal – on her 18th birthday, no less – with Arsenal's Jordan Nobbs getting the second. England under-19s won 2–0. This was a landmark for women's football in England – the first major tournament that any of our teams would win. Duggan and Nobbs would soon progress through to become regulars in the full international side, as would fellow winners Lucy Bronze and Jade Moore, and for me that was so satisfying. The team kept clean sheets throughout the tournament, and goalie Rebecca Spencer and defender Chelsea Weston were both named among the ten 'emerging talents' of the tournament by UEFA. The structure that we'd all worked so hard to put in place from the grassroots up was really beginning to bear fruit.

Another good indication of the progress that we were making in English women's football was in the more professional make-up of our senior squad for Finland. Six of the players were earning a full-time living in the professional American league, our goalie Rachel Brown coached on Everton's community scheme, Faye White was a community officer at Arsenal, Fara Williams was working as an FA skills coach, midfielder Jill Scott was coaching in the community, and there were a number of players who were already earning part or all of their living from football. And now we had central contracts.

But controversy also shrouded my squad selection for Finland, as for any football manager it almost always will. After much thought, I'd decided not to select one of our senior players, Rachel Yankey, for the tournament. She had not been playing well, and though I have a lot of time for Yanks, her levels of performance didn't justify me including her in the squad. I know she was bitterly disappointed. But from day one, as a manager, I have always let my players know that no one is indispensable. Kelly Smith and Faye White were both selected by me, though they were both coming back from injuries; Faye was the ultimate leader on the pitch, Kelly, a world-class striker. When you have players who can turn – or save – a game, you think long and hard about leaving them out. It's the gamble that all international managers have to take. But after getting extensive advice from Pippa and the fitness team, I decided we could manage both their situations through the tournament.

Our opening group C game in Lahti was against Italy – a country who had twice been European Championship runners-up in the late nineties but, by 2009, had become a shadow of their former selves. Along with Russia, they were regarded as the group outsiders. The first half felt like the archetypical opening tournament game – cagey, both sides testing one another out. Fara scored a penalty just before half-time and all was looking comfortable. But then disaster struck. Casey Stoney was adjudged to have pushed the Italian Melania Gabbiadini and, to everyone's shock, she was sent off.

The Italians pressed forward more in the second half and goals from Patrizia Panico and Alessia Tuttino sealed a 2–1 win for the Italians. On paper, our opening game was our easiest, and we'd lost it. Next up were Russia, who again, everyone expected us to beat – and we had to, to stay in the tournament. Whether or not the pressure of expectation got to the girls, I will never know. But their first 20 minutes against the Russians in the Finnair Stadium was up there with the worst I had ever seen England play under my management. The players were anxious and in their shells, constantly giving the ball away. After only two minutes, our defence melted and Ksenia Tsybutovich stepped in to put the Russians one up. A second from Oleysa Kurochkina came nearly 20 minutes later. Not even half an hour into the first half and we were 2–0 down and looking like frightened rabbits. Nearly two hours into the tournament and we'd offered very little.

It may be a cliché to say that goals change games, but it's true – particularly well-timed ones. A minute later Karen Carney threw us a lifeline with a strike through the keeper's legs into the far corner, and suddenly the whole complexion of the game began to change. We started to keep the ball, passes went to feet and, as though they had awoken from a deep slumber, players began to galvanise themselves and suddenly looked alert, firing on all cylinders. Their confidence renewed, the team started to run at the Russian defence and, a few minutes later, Eni Aluko grabbed the equaliser. Just before half-time, Kelly Smith scored a peach to put us 3–2 in front. The Russian goalie kicked a poor clearance that landed right at Kelly's feet. She looked up, and then from 40 yards out, audaciously lobbed the keeper. After one of the most Jekyll and Hyde halves of football I'd ever seen, we went in at half-time in front. With no more goals in what was a steady England second-half performance, the final whistle blew with us running out 3–2 winners.

Coming back from 2–0 down in any major tournament is some achievement, and it seemed to do something to the squad's overall self-confidence. We went into our final group match against potentially our toughest opponents, Sweden, needing a point to qualify for the last eight. We'd only beaten Sweden once in our last nine meetings, and thus far in the tournament the Scandinavians had not conceded a goal. Sweden invariably played 4–4–2 and, throughout the team, were big and strong. We knew they'd offer a real physical challenge. So, similar to our game against them in the 2005 Euros, I asked the girls to take a deep line in defence and compete in every area. We were a smaller, less physical team, so needed to make up for it with our athleticism and pace. It was a tough ask, but the girls were really up for it. Clawing their way back from 2–0 down against the Russians had instilled a new sense of belief in themselves. They were starting to look battle-hardened.

Casey Stoney was available for the Sweden game after her sending off against Italy, and she would be the only change I would make from the Russia game, dropping Rachel Unitt to the bench. The team played with a measured poise and confidence that surprised the Swedes. Faye White, who once again won player of the match (as she did in so many of the big games), outjumped a Swedish defender and scored with a header on 28 minutes. Twelve minutes later, the ref decided that Katie Chapman had fouled Lotta Schelin in the box and Victoria Svensson scored from the penalty spot to make it 1–1. And that would be the final score: not only the point we needed to qualify for the quarter-finals, but an extremely honourable draw against one of the world's best sides. Defensively, we had been immense, Faye's performance was world-class. So it was on to the quarter-finals to meet Finland in Turku.

Playing the tournament hosts is never an easy task, and Finland were big, strong and dangerous in the air. I was relieved that we had Anita Asante back in the centre of defence alongside Faye, because I knew we would have to endure a long-ball aerial bombardment from the Finns. I was not wrong. Throughout the first half, the ball came flying in at us again and again. But despite all of the Finnish pressure, we defended with real resolution. Gradually, as the half went on, we began to create more of our own chances. Sue Smith chased down a poor backpass which Finland goalie Tinja-Riikka Korpela just managed to clear. But we quickly picked up possession again on the edge of their box, Fara Williams slipped a slide-rule pass through to Eniola Aluko, who calmly stroked it pass Korpela.

Late in the first half, disaster struck. Faye, who was putting in a towering performance yet again, went up to challenge for a ball with Finnish striker Sanna Talonen. There was a horrible clash of heads and Faye hit the ground like a sack of potatoes. She was clearly in a state. Pippa raced on to tend to her. I could tell from the shake of Pippa's head that it was not good news. Faye was stretchered off and Pippa sent her immediately for x-rays, scans and further treatment.

It was a really nasty injury. The accidental clash of heads had not only fractured her cheekbone but dislocated it too. For the rest of the game – perhaps the rest of the tournament – we would be without our influential skipper. I felt gutted for Faye. She'd fought back from a series of injuries to make it to the tournament. And when I saw the pain she was in, my heart began to race. But, as manager, I now needed to stay calm and concentrate on reorganising.

I brought on Jill Scott and we saw out the first half without conceding. After the break, the aerial bombardment continued as the Finns searched for an equaliser. Soon after the re-start, another long ball was flicked on by Linda Sällström for Talonen, whose shot was deflected wide by Asante. Minutes later, Jill Scott won a free-kick in their half. Sue Smith's centre was met at the far post by Chapman. Korpela could only parry the stinging shot and Fara Williams was in the right place at the right time to poke it home from close range. Two–nil up with 40 minutes to go.

Kelly Smith had a couple of near misses, the second a superb dipping 30-yard strike that flew just inches over the bar. We were well on top. But tournament football is all about keeping concentration. On 65 minutes, an in-swinging corner was headed goalwards by Sällström. Sue Smith blocked it on the line, but the ball fell to an unmarked Annica Sjölund, who rifled home a lifeline for the Finns.

What happened next made me feel extremely proud of my players. For years I had been preaching the importance of bouncing straight back after a setback, and not letting heads drop. It was exactly that sort of resilience that the best international teams showed time and again.

From the re-start, the ball was played out to Eniola, who showed a confident and forceful burst of speed to take her past three of their defenders. Demonstrating great close control and awareness, she buried an unstoppable shot past Korpela. Our two-goal advantage was restored.

But the Finns remained relentless. Asante, Laura Bassett and Scott put in immense performances at the back but, finally, the Scandinavians' high tempo, high-ball pressure got them back into the game. With just eight minutes to go, Maija Saari swung in a corner and Sällström reacted quickest to nod the loose ball home.

The partisan crowd became their twelfth woman, roaring them forward and creating an electric atmosphere in the stadium. Another Saari corner from the right was blocked on the line by Sue Smith and, after a huge goal-line scramble, Rachel Brown managed to safely gather. More corners followed, with goalie Korpela even coming up for one. It was nail-biting stuff, but we hung on. I was, of course, overjoyed that we'd won and were through to the semis – but, in truth, given the battering the Finns had given us in the last ten minutes, the overwhelming emotion was one of relief.

Our opponents in the last four would prove to be a surprise. Together, we all watched the other quarter-final live on TV. The heavily unfancied Holland played out an uneventful 0–0 draw against one of the perennial hot favourites, France, and then beat them on penalties. But the Dutch were no mugs, and we knew we'd be going into the semis without Faye on the pitch.

Immediately after the Finland game, we flew Faye back to England, to see Ian Hutchison, the surgeon who'd operated on John Terry's cheekbone, prior to him wearing a face mask for a Champion's League tie. The good news was that he felt he could do a similar procedure for Faye, and she was desperate to have the op and hopefully rejoin us if we could progress further in the tournament.

After so many weeks away from home, the staff and the players can feel like they're living in a bubble, so all the time we added to our a wall of inspiration, filling it with letters, good luck messages and press coverage, to make everyone aware of the support back home. The mood in the camp was buoyant, but it was a disappointment that more fans couldn't follow our exploits. Eurosport showed our games live, but it was a satellite channel and a lot of people didn't have satellite television. The BBC, ITV and Channels Four and Five showed nothing, not even highlights. So the terrestrial audience back home were badly neglected.

Holland coach Vera Pauw liked to play very defensively, so our training sessions concentrated on ways of breaking down the Dutch and getting behind their back four. We had not been short on goals since we arrived in Finland and had plenty of pace and movement in Eni, Kelly and Kaz, so I was very hopeful. It was at the back we'd been having our problems and, without Faye to lead the team, a lot of responsibility fell on Anita Asante and Lindsay Johnson, who was acting as Faye's replacement.

Thrilling though it was to be in the semi-finals of a major tournament, many of the girls were beginning to feel the aches, pains and strains that come with playing high-pressure games virtually every other day. The six players who were plying their trade in the USA had just come off a gruelling six-month season, and a number of the other girls were carrying knocks and bruises. Physio Tracy Lewis and Pippa and the rest of the medical team worked overtime to get the players match-ready, and we began to tweak the players' training and conditioning schedules to cater for each of their individual needs at the semi-final stage. In Faye's absence, I made Fara captain, which reflected my admiration for her growing maturity and strong leadership qualities.

From the off, Holland, as they say, parked the bus. Just as we expected, they weren't particularly fussed about how much possession they got, and defended en masse. Shots on goal were hard to come by, as every time we got one away, there was invariably a player in orange ready to block. It was a very impressive example of deep defending. We went in at half-time in a 0–0 stalemate.

I asked the players to try to get behind the Dutch defence as much as they could. After 60 minutes, we did just that and Kelly Smith rattled in a goal to put us 1–0 up. The Dutch response was immediate. Marlous Pieëte netted the equaliser just minutes later. They reverted to stifling and frustrating us and it ended up 1–1 at the end of normal time. For the second time in four days, the Netherlands were going into extra-time.

But on this occasion they didn't make it to penalties. Saving all the drama until last, and with just three minutes of extra-time left, Jill Scott powered home a header from a Karen Carney corner. It was the winner, 2–1, and we were through to the final of the Euros.

I'm not usually a big fan of what stats may or may not tell us, but the simple truth was we had 20 shots on target against Holland's five. We were more than worthy winners and, if the Dutch hadn't been at their deeply defensive best, I don't think it would have gone into extra-time.

For the rest of that night and for the next couple of days, you could sense a real feeling of relief among the players. All the hard work that went into preparing for the tournament, getting through the group stages and now into the final had resulted in an odd sense of euphoria, excitement and ... well, just sheer relief. That we'd managed to stay in the tournament right to the very end, to the very last game, was a fantastic achievement and showed just how far we'd come in the ten years since I'd been manager.

But a semi-final win is a classic case of 'so near yet so far'. You enjoy the celebration of the moment, but the minute we were back at the team hotel, we had a meeting with the players and the staff to begin planning for the final. It wasn't a case of me being a slave driver, because the gaps between games in the top women's tournaments are much shorter than in the men's game. We only had a couple of days before we were to meet the might of reigning European champions Germany. As we went into the 2009 final, the simple fact was that we had never ever beaten Germany. And, given their dominance in the game, it's perhaps easy to understand why. Germany were not only the reigning Euro champions, they'd won six out of the nine tournaments since its inception in 1984. Before Finland, they'd won the previous four finals. In 2005, they saw off Norway 3–1 in the final, after having won every single game along the way. They were also the reigning FIFA Women's World Cup holders, having won back-to-back titles in 2003 and 2007. Most of their squad had played in the 2007 tournament, including their striker Birgit Prinz, who was a three-time winner of FIFA's Women's World Player of the Year, and came into the Finland tournament having scored 123 goals for her country. In Silvia Neid, they had one of the most tactically astute and most successful women managers of all time. The task we had ahead of us was about as tough as it gets.

But this is why you want to become an international manager: to pit your wits against the very best. The very fact that we were in the final showed that we had earned the right to live among the world's best. And if we were to win trophies, it was the likes of Germany we needed to beat. We had come a long way. I was confident that our squad was the best England had, up until then, ever possessed.

Faye was back in the camp. In order to get used to her white protective face mask, she wore it around the hotel for a couple of days, and scared the life out of some of the other guests. The other girls were joking around with her and calling her 'Phantom of the Opera'. But I was just relieved she was back and seemingly happy with the protection the mask would give her.

Our other major injury worry continued to be Kelly. She'd suffered so many awful injuries throughout her career, and three months before the Euros had damaged her knee playing in the US for the Boston Breakers. From day one of arriving in Finland, we tailored Kelly's training schedule to her fitness needs, to accommodate her many sessions in the physio's room. After the semi-final, the team were working on Kelly's knee until midnight.

We had a light-hearted quiz one night in the hotel, and Faye and Kelly were asked which one of them was nicknamed 'Sicknote'. Each gave the other as their answer. Some people criticised me at the time for taking players who were carrying injuries. But when you're in a big tournament you desperately need your biggest players. Faye and Kelly were two of our most experienced and consistent performers. This was Germany's sixth Euros final. It was our first, in the modern era. The German players had earned hundreds of caps between them, so our most experienced players were key to the final. We were used to managing Kelly's injuries and, as long as she felt able to play, we wanted her there with us.

The players didn't need motivating, far from it. But just for good measure I let them know that Silvia Neid's backroom team had already booked a restaurant in Helsinki to throw their celebration dinner. And they'd also had winners' t-shirts printed. This didn't go down well with my players at all. In fact, it really riled some of them. There was much chuntering about the arrogant Germans showing us no respect, and people were getting really fired up. Job done.

I remember thinking how much I would love the day to arrive when myself and the England squad could set ourselves such consistently high standards and be so supremely confident in our own abilities that we too might book our celebrations before a final even kicked off. In Britain, that's called tempting fate, which says a lot about our culture. The fate that Germans tempt is called success.

Before the final we received a letter from David Cameron wishing us luck, video messages from David Beckham, Wayne Rooney and John Terry, plus texts and phone calls from Steven Gerrard, David James, Sir Trevor Brooking and Stuart Pearce. We were also given a great boost by the news that the BBC had given in to criticism back home and bought the terrestrial rights to screen the final live.

That was like a victory in itself – we were so keen to share the excitement of us making it to a European Championship final with football fans back in England. After having been live on terrestrial TV for every single one of our Euro 2005 matches, it had been a big disappointment that the major channels had passed on covering us in 2009. It felt like all the progress we had been making in getting more coverage and prominence for the women's game in England had stalled somewhat. So this was great news.

The night before the final I was up until the wee small hours going over checklists with the staff and players. Was everybody happy? Had we missed anything? Did everyone have enough information about the German team and the way they played? Or had I given them too much? One thing was for sure. We were going to attack. If we sat back, I knew we'd be in trouble. I put Eni on the left, because although the German back four was a formidable unit, I thought Eni had more pace than Linda Bresonik on their right. The Germans had precious few chinks in their armour, but this I thought was one of them that we could exploit. I put Kelly in the centre and Karen Carney out on the right, so that we had real pace up front, that we could go back to front as quickly as possible. I spoke to the players collectively and individually, making sure they were each completely certain what their roles would be and how to approach their own personal battles with the German players on the pitch. We were ready and prepared.

The final was to be inside the historic Helsinki Stadium, which hosted the 1952 summer Olympics. It's regarded as one of the most architecturally beautiful sports stadiums in the world, and was also home to the Finland men's and women's national football teams. It was a fitting venue for what I hoped would be our finest hour. In the coach on the way to the ground there was a crackle of excitement among the players and the back-up team. Our captain Faye was back and ready for selection and the intense work that the medical team had done on Kelly's knee since the semi-final game meant she too was fit to play. My starting line up was: Rachel Brown, Casey Stoney, my captain Faye White, Anita Asante, Alex Scott, Jill Scott, Fara Williams, Katie Chapman, Karen Carney, Kelly Smith and Eniola Aluko.

The final was played on a balmy September night, and for the first 20 minutes, our game-plan worked well. We started brightly, took the game to Germany, pinned them back and enjoyed most of the possession. Eni Aluko's pace was really putting their defence on the back foot and Kelly Smith's movement had them bemused. But then came six minutes when the world went mad.

Against the run of play, Inka Grings span a pass into the box and predator Birgit Prinz poked home her first goal of the tournament (it hadn't quite been happening for Birgit in Finland, but the very best usually come good in the big games). Two minutes later, Melanie Behringer took a steadying touch over 40 yards out and then fizzed a stunning shot into the top corner of Rachel Brown's net. An unbelievable strike and one of the best I've ever seen before or since in a final. Now it was vital that we didn't buckle. And thanks to Kelly Smith, we didn't. Two minutes later she picked up a ball just outside the left-hand corner of their box, dribbled it past two German defenders and then slipped a pass across to Karen Carney who slotted in from five yards out. On a day when so many critics had been talking about Germany's many world-class performers, Kelly showed once again why she was regarded in the same company.

Two minutes later, Fara Williams lashed a shot just past the angle of post and crossbar from 20 yards out. On 36 minutes, a Jill Scott header was cleared off the German line. Half-time came, and we were still very much in it. I gave the girls advice about how to continue dealing with their own personal battles

170

across the pitch. But the general message was, 'More of the same, please.' We were more than matching the Germans in every department. The girls were quick to the ball and, crucially, kept hold of it once we'd won it.

Five minutes into the second half Germany won a corner. We failed to clear it. Annike Krahn's shot cannoned against the base of the post and Kim Kulig slammed in the rebound. But, once again, we bounced back. Karen Carney found Kelly Smith in the box. With a superbly deft left-foot touch, she flicked the ball past a German defender and powered a viciously swinging drive into the far-right corner of the goal past Nadine Angerer's despairing left hand.

We'd shown real battling qualities in coming back from 2–0 down against Russia, and you could tell that, as we threatened again, the English fans in the crowd were starting to wonder if history was about to repeat itself. It was not to be. Five minutes later came the killer blow. Kerstin Garefrekes wriggled down the right and whipped over a cross that Inka Grings headed over Rachel Brown.

The glut of goals must have been great for the fans to watch. For me, they were torture. We now had under 25 minutes to get back into the game and I had to decide whether or not to make changes. I decided against. The German goals had been special. But my team were playing well.

What separates the sides at the very top of the pile from the rest is that they play with total intensity for 90 minutes. Their concentration and focus is such that they hardly ever switch off. The last 25 minutes would be a measure of how far we had come together as a squad, whether or not we deserved to be winners. But the pressure proved too much and we switched off.

Suddenly, passes started going astray. We couldn't find the out balls to Eni, Kelly or Kaz Carney and things began to unravel. I have so much admiration for Silvia Neid and the succession of great teams she'd put together, and though I didn't like what happened next one little bit, I couldn't help but take my hat off to the Germans. Where a lot of other teams in a major final may well have settled for the two-goal cushion of 4–2 and closed the game down, they smelt blood and went for the kill. With 18 minutes to go, it was two on two on the edge of our box. Unfortunately for us, the German 'two' were Birgit Prinz and Inka Grings. Prinz expertly tee-ed up Grings and her left-foot strike made it 5–2. Three minutes later, Grings returned the favour and became Prinz's provider. She rattled an unstoppable right-foot shot past Rachel Brown. The game was up.

A lot of the critics thought that the 6–2 scoreline didn't reflect how close much of the game had been. But the truth is, we matched the Germans well for 60 minutes or so. Then we switched off. When you do that against the very best sides, then you lose.

Should I have changed tactics? Definitely not. Put some fresh legs on earlier? I believed the best 11 players were on the pitch. But isn't hindsight a wonderful thing? I could have brought three new faces on after the fourth goal, but that could also have upset the balance and momentum of the players already on the pitch. In such a high-pressure, high-tempo game, it can be hard for subs to come on and immediately get up to speed with the nature of the game. At 4–2 down, I looked at the players on our bench and then at the players on theirs. We were not strong enough. Their squad had so much more depth than ours. I discovered after the game, that, at 4–2, Silvia Neid was having very different thoughts. She told me that she still felt uncomfortable – that the way we were playing, we could still have got back in the game. She wasn't happy until they had scored their fifth.

So we were runners-up, silver medallists. In so many ways, it was England's best ever achievement and I was so proud of how well the girls had played for one another throughout the tournament. Kelly and Eni both ended the tournament as second-equal top scorers with three goals each, and we'd put in some brave performances to get all the way into the final.

But I have never liked coming second. We'd put down a marker and got a podium finish. Now I was already thinking about the 2011 World Cup and how we could take what we'd learnt in Finland, to go that one step further. Personally, I wasn't overly enamoured with second place and the silver medal. I refused to touch it for a while, and it's now in the National Football Museum in Manchester, along with my Euro boots.

At the start of the game, I'd noticed a banner in the crowd that read 'England Neid-Mare', obviously referring to the German coach Silvia Neid. It was somewhat prophetic. For although we played brightly in the first half and into the second, the numbers did tell their own story – Germany 6 England 2. For the seventh time in ten tournaments, the Germans were once more champions of Europe. I am not a jealous person – envy is a waste of energy – but watching Silvia lead her joyous players around the Helsinki Olympic stadium holding the Cup aloft, I couldn't help but think, 'Damn, I wish that was us.'

Chapter 14

No Hope

Early one cold dark morning in October 2009, I was waiting for an FA car to come and pick me up from my house in south London. We were going to drive north to Blackpool for England's first qualifying group match for the 2011 World Cup. I idly checked my phone, and discovered that, overnight, I'd been sent a series of voice messages and texts. Most of them, from one of the FA's PR guys, Johan. I opened the first one. Johan was asking what did I know about a meeting with Grimsby Town football club? I actually wondered if he'd had a few. The message made absolutely no sense at all. I had no idea what it could have related to.

My car arrived bang on time. So I put the mobile away and resolved to listen to the rest of the messages when I got into my hotel in Blackpool. I had more important things to worry about than what garbled messages may or may not mean. I was concentrating hard on how I would prepare the squad for the Malta game. After so recently crossing swords with the likes of Germany, Spain and Holland this would be a totally different challenge.

It would be the first time we'd ever played Malta, for a start. But my scouting team, and video analyst Phil, had all done their homework. I knew their coach Pierre Brincat would be putting out a hugely defensive formation, ready to pack their penalty area and fight for their lives. His side's last game had been against Spain and they were hammered 13–0. You didn't have to be an idiot to realise we were overwhelming pre-match favourites. But as a manager there's no such thing as an easy game: banana skins lie in wait around every corner for the complacent. Against smaller nations like Malta, it's as much about how you win, as getting the result.

There would be no Kelly Smith, who was injured. I rested a lot of my first-choice players like Karen Carney and Eni Aluko, as I had decided to give some of the younger players more international experience. It was a chance to see how the coming generation would perform.

I booked into the team hotel and decided to take a shower to wake me up. I came back into my room in a dressing gown and switched on the BBC news. There on the screen was some old TV footage of me on the touchline at an England match, plus the news that I had been spotted in a restaurant talking animatedly with the chairman of League Two Grimsby Town Football Club, John Fenty, and that I was considering becoming the Mariners' new manager, in line to replace the recently sacked Mike Newell. According to press reports, I had formally applied for the position. In other words, I would potentially be the first woman to become boss of a professional English football club.

The irony of this was that Newell had got himself into hot water a few years previously, when manager at Luton, for slagging off the assistant referee Amy Rayner and generally questioning the very idea that women should have any role in men's football. He was reported at the time as saying that the appointment of women referees and assistants was 'tokenism for the politically correct idiots'. It should be pointed out that he later unreservedly apologised for his remarks. But he certainly said what a lot of men in the game thought.

The other irony was that England's first women's football team was allegedly formed in Grimsby back in 1886. Nine years before the British (London) Ladies Club, who were once thought to be the original pioneers of the women's game. So this Grimsby Town development was interesting news.

Back on the screen, one of the BBC *Breakfast Time* presenters invited me into the studio, if I was watching, to explain what was happening. Hilarious!

There were only three things wrong with the story. One, I'd only ever been to Grimsby once in my life, and that was for a World Cup qualifier back in 2001. Two, I'd never met John Fenty. And three, I hadn't applied for the job. Apart from that, they did manage to spell my name right. The headline on the back page of the *Sun* was 'HOPE SPRINGS FOR GRIMSBY'. The truth is there was no Hope.

To this day I still don't have a clue who concocted the story or the reason why. Some have suggested that the club dreamt up the idea to get some column inches. Others, that it was one of the tabloids having a slow news day. Either way, it really was a load of old rubbish. But it proved to be a pain in the backside because I was trying to prepare for an England game, while there was this whole circus going on around me.

The League Managers Association chief executive Richard Bevan was quoted on air, saying, 'Why shouldn't she make the step into the men's game? Hope has done a fantastic job with England, but I'm not sure the FA would want to let her go.' I began to realise why I'd had so many voice messages, particularly from the FA! Not surprisingly, they wanted to know what the heck was going on.

I went down to hotel reception and this guy suddenly appeared from nowhere and introduced himself: 'I'm [so and so] and I'm from the *Sun*. Is it true you're gonna be Grimsby manager?' I rolled my eyes and walked back off to the lift to go back to my room. But Mr So and So was right at my shoulder, following me.

'Are you going up?' I asked him.

He nodded. So when the lift doors opened, I beckoned him in first: 'After you.'

I stayed put where I was, the lift doors closed and the *Sun* reporter disappeared. For ever. Well, from my life.

I rang Michelle to tell her what was happening. But she already knew because the press were camped outside our home in south London. As usual, Michelle went off very early in the morning on her bicycle to open up the sandwich shop. She turned the corner of our front wall, and discovered a news reporter and a cameraman, crouched waiting. The reporter, who clearly didn't know football, thought Michelle was me. As she cycled off down the street, he was trying to keep up alongside, firing questions at her. It was totally mad.

I answered Johan's calls and told him there was not one grain of truth to the story. The head of the FA's security, Ray Whitworth, was absolutely brilliant. He said if we needed security outside our house, to just ring. And, similarly, Yvonne McLaughlin, who was in charge of the team's security, offered any and every help she could. Throughout my time at the FA both Ray and Yvonne were consistently brilliant to work with.

Actually, I found the whole Grimsby Town saga pretty hilarious. But it did show how much under the microscope a woman would be if she took over a professional men's team in Britain. Just the hint that I might have applied for the job filled out the back pages of most of the tabloids and quite a few columns in the broadsheets.

You just have to look at the media circus that surrounded Helena Costa when she was appointed boss at Ligue 2 Clermont Foot in France in 2014. Helen's a great professional coach. She's got her UEFA A licence, she's coached Benfica's youth team and scouted for Celtic in Spain and Portugal. It didn't work out for her in Clermont-Ferrand because of disagreements with the board, and she quit after a month or so. But for a while she was front and back page news all over the world. Interestingly, her successor was another woman, former French international Corinne Diacre, who's still there as manager.

Would the huge scrutiny I would undoubtedly come under stop me if I was offered a similar job? I doubt it. Throughout my career, as player, manager and coach, my feeling has always remained the same. If I am offered an opportunity that looks even half interesting, then I will seriously consider it. And if that included managing a men's team, then so be it. It's all football.

At the time, I was correctly quoted in the *Daily Telegraph* as saying, 'I think the world of football has to accept that women are qualified to be part of the game. We have some fantastic female coaches, not only in England but across the world, and we should be respected for putting in the work to gain these qualifications. Sometimes I'm not sure we get that credit.' That's a few years ago, but I still stand by every word, because progress in women's football in this country – and the perception of it – still moves slowly.

What very few people know is that in 2012 I was approached by Windsor FC to become their manager, and I did seriously look at the offer. At the time Windsor had finished as runners-up in the Combined Counties Football League Premier Division, having been set up in the summer of 2011 from the ashes of Windsor and Eton FC.

OK, so I knew they weren't a professional league team. But they had a chairman who was very innovative, go-ahead and gender blind. We met, we talked, and I liked him and his vision for the club. I did really contemplate it. But, at the time, I was on a roller coaster of 2012 Olympics, World Cup and preparation for the European Championships with England and GB, and the opportunity went away. The timing just wasn't right. But who knows what the future might bring? Why shouldn't well-qualified women manage in the men's game?

The problem is, it always becomes some sort of ridiculous oppositional thing, based solely on gender. It's never represented in the media as: are Helena Costa, Hope Powell or even Silvia Neid individually well equipped or good enough as individuals to coach or manage a men's team? It's only ever portrayed as a boring reactionary blanket statement: is a woman good enough to coach a top men's team? Of course, a good number of women are more than capable.

I would love to see managers and coaches like Carolina Morace, Vera Pauw or Hesterine de Reus, who have flair, ability, great management skills and experience, take over at a few men's clubs across Europe and beyond. Because the less thoughtful areas of the press would make it simply a matter of gender, they would absolutely be in the goldfish bowl and under constant, questioning scrutiny. But each of the aforementioned are more than good enough to manage across the levels in women's *and* men's football. Management isn't a gender issue, it's about capabilities.

Let me just turn the tables a little on that thought. Why are there still so many men who are managers and coaches in the women's game? I'll be honest, I think quite a few of them are just not good enough to coach and manage in the men's game. But because they're men, and because the system has been run by men for so many years, I think they get an easier route into women's football. Increasingly, there are more and more women who are qualified, who have all their badges and are out and out football people. So why aren't they being given the jobs in the women's game?

At international level, around the time I was replaced by Mark Sampson in 2013, a number of other countries – France, Holland, Canada and Australia – replaced their women managers with men. What message is this putting out to the women who are working so hard to get on in the game?

My real worry is that great coaching prospects like Casey Stoney, Fara Williams, Kelly Smith, et al., will be put off by the lack of opportunities and be lost to TV and media work. Great though they would all be in those areas, it would be a tragic loss to women's football. But currently, only three of our 19 WSL teams have a woman manager – if this continues, where do they go to hone their craft at the highest domestic level?

Don't get me wrong. There are many very able and talented men in the women's game, who I personally have a lot of respect for. They've given a lot to the sport. And some of my greatest inspirations and friends – Alan May, Howard Wilkinson and Stuart Pearce, for instance – are obviously men. But it's vital that women's football gets more and more female coaches and managers. It has always been my mission – and always will be – to do everything I can to make that happen. In over 40 years of

England women's football I remain the only woman to manage the national team, and that's just not right.

It's not like women's football in this country is a minority sport. According to an FA survey carried out in 2011, women's football – played regularly by 1.4 million across England – is the third largest team sport in the country, after men's football and men's cricket. If there are so many women involved in playing the sport, why shouldn't more be coaching and managing?

We beat Malta 8–0 at Bloomfield Road and it should have been 20, to be honest. Malta didn't help themselves either. Their central defender Natasha Pace got herself sent off after 57 minutes. Fara Williams scored a hat-trick. Three points under our belts, we were up and running in the qualifying campaign for the 2011 World Cup.

Chapter 15

Top Ten

Big things were expected of us in Germany for the 2011 World Cup tournament. We went into the competition full of confidence, having recently beaten highly ranked Sweden and World Cup favourites USA in friendly games. The latter match, though a wonderful confidence-boosting 2–1 win against one of the top table teams in the world, brought to the fore a problem I was experiencing within the FA.

A new project called Club England had been launched in the building. Les Reed had conceived the original idea, as a way of players and, particularly, supporters to feel like they were part of a club, not just a national side. That kind of died a death. But a new version of Club England was launched, helmed by Adrian Bevington, and was quite different in concept. His Club England gathered together the senior men's manager, coaches and admin staff to talk regularly about budgets, operational matters and fixture calendars. Myself and the then under-21 boss Stuart Pearce were initially not invited.

I put in a request for the finance and logistics required to arrange what I considered was a very important friendly against the USA. It was important for us as a challenge, because in our preparation for the 2011 World Cup, apart from perhaps

Germany, there was no team in the world except the USA who considered every single game as a must-win, do or die event. So-called 'friendly' or otherwise, I was told that a Club England meeting had decided there was a shortfall in funding and the friendly couldn't be justified.

I went to Adrian and told him I was annoyed that this decision had been made by Club England at meetings I'd hadn't been invited to. He told me under-21 boss Stuart Pearce hadn't been invited either. I said I couldn't give a shit. If it meant deciding on money I needed for my women's teams, I wanted to be there. I fought for and won the money that would make that very important friendly happen. But not being invited to this new Club England venture really pissed me off. It was a depressing indication that, no matter what great progress I thought we'd made in the women's game – changing hearts and minds within the FA – it still wasn't thought necessary for the overall manager to be invited to this new structure of meetings. I made bloody sure I was invited to their meetings in the future. As it was, the USA match was a massively valuable experience for the players. To get to play one of the world's leading nations before a major tournament was the best possible preparation. We all knew that the USA were hardwired to win, friendly or not, so it would be a great test for us. We won 2–1 and were worthy winners. A key to the victory was playing Fara Williams in a pivotal central midfield role. Throughout the game, she quickly sprayed the ball wide out on the wings to Jess Clarke and Rachel Yankey, both of whom scored our two first-half goals. Not many sides beat the USA, and it was a massive confidence booster. It taught a number of my younger players that not only could we live with the best, we could beat them.

At the World Cup we were drawn in group B, alongside Mexico, Canada and New Zealand, which many critics regarded as a comparatively easy group. But although the squad I'd picked for Germany was a powerful one, the standard of the women's game was improving all the time. The gap between the very best and the rest was narrowing.

People pointed to Mexico's world ranking of 25th to suggest that our opening group match would be a foregone conclusion. I knew differently. This was the team who had beaten the USA in qualifying for the World Cup proper. They had some handy ball players and a top, experienced coach in Leo Cuéllar who, like me, had been in the job since 1998. Having had them watched by my scouts six or seven times, I realised they would be a real handful.

To begin with we were based in Wolfsburg which, thanks to the huge Volkswagen factory there, is the richest city in Germany. I'd travelled to Wolfsburg before the World Cup to do a recce for our hotel and plumped for the Ritz-Carlton, which was an incredibly elegant building just a stone's throw from the VW plant. It had a three-star Michelin restaurant and a well-equipped conference room, which we took over for the duration of our stay, for team meetings, research and planning.

Wolfsburg was a city building quite a footballing pedigree. In 2009, the Wolfsburg men's team won the Bundesliga, and the women's team were developing into Germany's best. In 2013 and 2014 they would win the UEFA Women's Championship League and a brace of German league titles. It was a city that supported its football, and they turned out in numbers for all the group matches that were played there.

I will always remember Wolfsburg, too, as the city in which I had one of my most soul-searching moments as a football manager. Well before our first group game, we'd arranged for the players to visit the Volkswagen museum and factory for a bit of fun and distraction. I decided not to go and did some prep for our opening match back in my hotel room. I sat down, caught my reflection in the mirror, and couldn't stop staring. I looked so tired. All at once, 12 years of tournament after tournament, being in charge of all five women's teams, trying to develop the National Academy, the constant battles to make change happen, the long days and nights, being the public face of England women's football, it all came crashing down on me. I'd been doing the job of three or four people and I was absolutely knackered, physically and mentally. I hadn't really realised it until that moment, and everything began to cave in on me. I started talking to my reflection: 'Right, Hope, do you want to be here or don't you? I don't really know if I can do this any more. You have to think, make a decision. Do you really want to go through with this? Because if it's "yes" you've got to say so now and then you have to go again, and give this tournament 110 per cent. Or if you are going to say "no", then make the decision now.'

I stared for what seemed like a long time into the mirror and decided it had to be 'yes'. I couldn't give in, not after everything I'd sacrificed and all the battles I'd fought. I left my hotel room to get a breath of fresh air and, as I closed the door behind me, I put a lid on my doubts and promised myself that, no matter how knackered I felt, I would give the tournament my all.

The pressure that's on a manager is immense. It's 24/7, particularly at a tournament. Have you done enough research? Enough homework? Have you picked the right players, and are they all up for it? Are your tactics right? Have you been able to make all of your players understand what's required of them? Are they happy? Are *you* happy? Well, no, you never are. There's always something to improve, work harder on. Left-field problems that blindside you.

Despite the wonderful support I got from my staff, at the end of the day you're alone in your room. And you know that today, tomorrow, always, you're the point at the top of the pyramid and the buck always stops with you. I accept pressure and I think I deal with it well. But every now and again, you find yourself feeling a bit exhausted by it all.

I wasn't the only person in the camp suffering a bit of a crisis. Prior to the World Cup, Kelly Smith once again had to fight her way back from a string of injuries, and she'd lost some faith in herself. I got our analyst Phil to edit together some really positive clips of her and then set it to music to give it some pizzazz. I said to Kelly, 'I want you to watch this. This is how good you are. And you need to remind yourself of just how good you are.' She needed to feel like she was a good player again. What I've always loved about Kelly is that she's so humble. She was never arrogant or played the superstar – even though she was one – but sometimes that lack of arrogance could be her Achilles heel. But we set about building her up again.

A player who'd bounced back from a crisis or two was Rachel Yankey. She had shown what spirit she had by returning to the squad after being dropped for the 2009 Euros. She'd been on great form and was showing a really great attitude again. I was very happy to have her back in the team.

I have to say it was one of my best ever squads, on and off the pitch. It was full of characters and the players were great at keeping one another upbeat. Jill Scott was the real character of the team

– crude, rude and witty. The other girls nicknamed her 'Crouch' because of her lankiness and she was always at the centre of banter and pranks in the hotel, in the dressing room and on the bus. She's a big Sunderland fan and her Wearside accent just seemed a perfect fit for comedy and one-liners. Fara Williams was a non-stop chatterer and a bit hyperactive, so we always had to keep her preoccupied. Then there were the more reflective individuals: Karen Bardsley was a good artist and was always drawing in her sketchbook; Casey Stoney loved her Martina Cole and Mo Hayder crime novels, and her case was always full of books. Anita Asante was doing a PhD in Network Policy and Women's Football and she'd spend her down time studying. Eni Aluko was studying to become a lawyer.

What all the girls shared in 2011 was a love of Twitter. They all had iPods and iPads, and while we were in Germany tweeted to their followers regularly. After our first group game in Germany, that would pose a bit of a problem, but more of that later.

By the time the Mexico game came around, the girls were champing at the bit. We'd had a week training get-together in Leicester before flying out, and then a week in Germany itself before the group began. It rained a lot in Wolfsburg, and although the players managed to fill their time with pool, table tennis and card games between the training, they were desperate to just get out on the pitch.

Keen though they were, as is so often the case with tournament opening games the players had a nervy start. But we had the lion's share of possession, and on 21 minutes our pressure paid off. Karen Carney whipped over a pinpoint delivery which was met by Fara Williams' forehead. Her looping header gave the Mexican goalie no chance.

We continued to dominate but, against the run of play, Mexico grabbed an unlikely equaliser. In the 33rd minute, Mónica Ocampo launched a speculative lob towards our goal. Karen Bardsley scrambled backwards but it crept in past her. Karen and the rest of us were bitterly disappointed. It should never have gone in, and the irony was that we'd talked to the players about trying to test the Mexican goalie from distance. At 16, Cecilia Santiago was totally inexperienced and the youngest keeper to play in either a men's or women's international tournament.

The equaliser galvanised Mexico, who dug in with real tenacity. We maintained an edge in both possession and territory, but Eni missed two great opportunities to put us back in the lead. First, missing the ball entirely from six yards out, and then shooting wide from a clever Kelly Smith cutback. In the last ten minutes, Kelly too went close, failing to get on the end of a dangerous cross whipped in by Ellen White. Mexico held out and we started off our group campaign with a single point.

I was quite prepared for press disappointment, but was not really expecting a problem that came right out of left field, from social media. Eni, who was a big Twitter user, received some poisonous tweets slagging her off for how she'd played. In my experience, this was new to women's football in England. Eni was really angry about the whole thing, and the players all rallied round her. That was typical of the squad we had; they all knew it had upset Eni. I was, as ever, blessed with such a supportive and empathetic team in Rachel Pav, Pippa and all the rest: they just concentrated on keeping the squad focused, happy and generally used this annoyance as another motivational tool.

We were all learning what a double-edged sword social media could be. On the one hand, it was testament to how popular the women's game was becoming in England that so many fans wanted to follow our players on Twitter and Facebook. And, in turn, it was good that our players had a relationship with the fans. But, on the other, it had caused an upset in the camp that we – and particularly Eni – could have done without. I don't think social media users realise just how damaging the remarks they make to players can be. Yes, of course everyone's entitled to an opinion, but when you've perhaps not had your best game in an England shirt you know it yourself, without having to read a hail of hurtful criticism condemning your performance. It's no coincidence that Eni has been a regular in the England team since she was a teenager, and you don't keep getting picked if you're not top international class. All players have off days. When fans become so bitter about it, naturally it has an effect.

We rolled on to Dresden to play New Zealand. It was a coach journey of just over 150 miles, and we were like a little wagon train, with vehicles travelling on in front of us that contained tons of equipment and personal luggage. We settled into our new home, the Maritim Hotel, and then joined the New Zealand players and staff on the balcony of Dresden city hall to be introduced to the mayor. It was great to see that the city was really embracing having the World Cup in town, and it was a nice little diversion for the players.

Between training sessions, they also managed to get in some sightseeing around Dresden, which I am told is a beautiful and historic city. In truth, I didn't get to see much of it. As an international manager, although your passport is full of stamps from around the world, and you might constantly be visiting dozens of countries, you rarely see much of them. The great majority of your time is spent on the training pitch, in hotel conference and meeting rooms, discussing tactics. Then, when the players are out getting some very necessary rest and recreation, consulting with your backroom team or endlessly going over videos alone in your hotel room. As we started to get more media coverage, I had more and more press conferences and interviews to fulfil. So it was rare that I ever got time to do any sightseeing as England manager. The focus was always on the next game.

The New Zealand manager John Herdman handed us a good motivational tool when he came out in the press and said he much preferred the idea of playing England than Japan because we were so boringly predictable. Press cuttings of that quote went up on the team wall and helped further fire up the girls.

For the New Zealand fixture, I made one change from the Mexico match, replacing Karen Carney with Ellen White, who played as a lone striker, with Eni switched to the right wing. As with the Mexico game we had more of the early possession, but then a couple of defensive lapses led to New Zealand taking the lead. Uncharacteristically, Faye White misjudged a long ball down the left flank, which let Amber Hearn in. She delivered a sweet cross which our central defence failed to deal with, leaving Sarah Gregorious free to tap in from close range.

To say that New Zealand were physical would be an understatement. They kicked lumps out of our flair players like Kelly Smith and Rachel Yankey, who didn't get much protection at all from the match officials.

At half-time I decided to bring Karen Carney on to replace Eni, who was having another indifferent game, in the hope that her skill and precision would worry the Kiwi defence. But it was New Zealand who started the second half the brighter, with

Amber Hearn looping a header just over the bar after some more uncertain defending. The New Zealanders now started to rough up Karen as well as Kelly and Yanks, and I was not best pleased with their game-plan.

But we soon got our own back in the most positive of ways. On the hour mark we were back in it. Alex Scott flighted a cross on to Jill Scott's head, who buried it past their goalie. With a few minutes to go, I brought on Jess Clarke. Minutes later she took a pass from Jill Scott inside the box and confidently cracked it into the top of the net. We held on to run out 2–1 winners. Four points in the bag, next up Japan.

After taking advice from Pippa and her team, I had to make the decision to rest Faye and Fara because of recent knee injuries they were carrying. The hope was we'd get through and they'd be fit for the quarter-finals. Pippa and I had become good friends since she first took up the post ten years previously, but our relationship as team manager and team doctor increasingly took on a slightly different pattern. I would consult with her over injuries to players. She would say something like, 'Kelly [or Faye, or whoever] can cope with 45 minutes in the next game.' And I would try to push it and negotiate, say, 60 minutes. What you have to understand is that Pippa has a 'friend voice' and a 'doctor voice'. At times like these she would use her ever so slightly sharper 'doctor voice' and deliver an emphatic 'no'. And I always listened, because at the end of the day the health and well-being of the players had to come first.

I trusted Pippa implicitly and over a period of years. She, along with physio Tracy Lewis, did an incredible job in shepherding the likes of Kelly and Faye through injuries and the rehab. The players loved both of them because they were the real deal and always looked after their best interests, health and fitness wise.

For the Japan game, I felt we had more physicality and strength and had to turn that to our advantage. They didn't have many weaknesses, but I identified that their two centre-backs were the most vulnerable area of the team. I told my players to sit back and let Japan play out from the back: 'When they get through midfield, go aggressive. Make big tackles and then go central on the counter, as early as possible.'

For Faye and Fara, I had two more than able replacements in Sophie Bradley and Anita Asante. And it was thanks to Sophie's long throws that we got our first genuine chance of the game. She sent in a skier that Ellen White nearly turned in, but Japanese defender Saki Kumagai turned it out for a corner.

Both sides played good possession football, but the breakthrough came for us after 15 minutes. Karen Carney looped a ball between Japan's two central defenders, Faye White deftly controlled it and sent a volleyed lob over the head of Japan's keeper Ayumi Kaihori.

At half-time I decided to bring on Rachel Yankey, and after 66 minutes she became the star of the show, doubling our lead with a clinical finish. She controlled a left-wing cross with one touch and then clipped the ball over the Japanese goalie's head. Though Japan continued to create a lot of movement and neat approach work, we shut them out to win 2–0. I was so pleased with the result. We were growing in confidence, trying different things. Sophie and Anita's performances at the centre of our defence showed that we now had a strong enough squad to bring players in who would do the business under pressure. We ended up top of our group and it was full steam ahead to the quarter-finals, where we were drawn against the French.

We flew to Düsseldorf, settled into the Hilton hotel and spent three days preparing for the big game. England were ranked tenth in the world, France were seventh. And though, over the years, we'd never beaten France in a major tournament, both teams were pretty equally matched. At its core, the French squad contained ten of the Olympique Lyonnais ladies' team that had won the Women's Champions League in 2010–11. They had a clutch of genuinely world-class players. But we were fresh from being finalists in the Euros and had a good number of flair players ourselves. Good though France were, my team and I felt we'd identified their major weakness. Down the centre was where we could break through. So I played Kelly right up front in the middle and put Jill Scott in behind her. Jill was brilliant at running late into the box.

I told the players that it was vitally important we were switched on right from the whistle, and we started really brightly. After 15 seconds Kelly latched on to a through ball, rounded the French keeper, Céline Deville, only for her shot to be blocked on the line by defender Laura Georges. As the first half progressed, the French gained more and more possession and were close to scoring on two or three occasions. But we rode the storm and went in at half-time 0–0.

I always had a policy of making no more than three points to the players at half-time. During the pressure of a big game, it's too much to expect the team to process and retain more than that. Also, I never went into the dressing room straight away. I'd let the players talk among themselves first and decompress a little from having been out on the pitch. Over the years, I increasingly tried to make half-time chat more and more player-led. Then I'd come in and give my three general points to the whole team and, if need be, talk individually to any players I felt could use a little more advice about their personal battles with opposition players.

During the France game, I basically asked for more of the same – more pressing, more movement and to keep concentration. Although France had had the better of the first half, we were playing OK. Even when we were playing badly, I tried to keep it as positive as possible. Over the years it was very rare that I ever lost it with the players at half-time. Maybe there were three or four occasions, but that was as near as I ever got to the legendary Fergie hairdryer treatment, because it wasn't my style, and I wasn't sure how much good it would have done anyway.

One tactical change I made at half-time against the French was to push Jill Scott a little further forward, and it worked for us. On 58 minutes she took advantage of a mix-up in the French defence and calmly flicked the ball over Deville's head. 1–0.

France came at us again and again, but we defended with real guts and bottle. So nearly there, but with three minutes of normal time to go the ball broke on the edge of the area for the lethal Élise Bussaglia to pounce and curl the ball past Karen Bardsley and into the top corner. 1–1. The players were gutted to get so near to the finishing line, but now I needed to lift them for 30 minutes of extra-time. I implored them to 'go again', forget the equaliser and get themselves a place in the semi-finals. It was still all up for grabs. The French were looking tired.

But so were we. Both sides had given so much during the regular 90 minutes that extra-time was often played at walking pace. Almost inevitably, extra-time ended without further score, and it all went down to penalties.

When I called the players round, I had to ask three times for volunteers before a single player put their hand up. I was amazed.

Where are you? And then the first player stepped forward – Claire Rafferty, a young kid who was making her international debut and had only been on the pitch for ten minutes. Then Kelly Smith, who could hardly walk, stepped forward. Faye and Casey followed, but still the others hung back. I can absolutely understand the nerves that some players must feel in that kind of situation, but I was disappointed that some of our more experienced players were so reluctant to put their hands up.

The shoot-out proved to be heart-stopping. We got off to a superb start when Camille Abily strode up to take France's first penalty and Karen Bardsley guessed correctly, dived to the right and guided the ball around the post. Kelly took our first pen and, with all her big-match temperament, sent a rocket into the top right-hand corner. The French scored their next two – Karen Carney and Casey Stoney both put their penalties away for us. We were 3–2 up. But then things began to unravel. Sonia Bompastor scored for them but, after being so brave to be the first to throw her hat into the ring, Claire Rafferty missed. I was gutted for her. We were back on level terms. Eugénie Le Sommer then put the French ahead, so it was all down to Faye White to keep us in it. She lashed in a powerful shot but, agonisingly, it rattled against the bar. We were out.

Immediately after the game, I had a conversation with Tony Leighton of the *Guardian* who, much credit to him, had really championed women's football in his newspaper's pages. I liked Tony as a person, and had trusted him. At the time, Tony was the only journalist whose number I had on my mobile phone. I told him, and I take full responsibility for saying it, that it felt like cowardice that my senior players hadn't put their hands up to take penalties. I said this in the heat of the moment, just minutes after we'd been knocked out. I was angry and disappointed. I didn't make it clear enough that it was an off-the-record comment to just him. But I did say this was a conversation I had to have with my players, behind closed doors. To my disappointment, Tony printed my remarks, pretty much out of context, I felt, and all hell broke loose. The world and his wife stepped forward to pass judgement on what I'd said. Every tabloid and broadsheet followed up on the story. I got absolutely slagged off in the press – how DARE I call my players cowards?

I know freelance journalists have to sell stories to make a living. And the more powerful those stories are, the better. But I was naïve in sharing my immediate, very emotional thoughts with Tony as a friend. It taught me an important lesson. No matter how well you know them, a journalist is never off-duty. Sadly, I could never trust Tony in the same way again, which I know upset him. It certainly upset me. I can completely understand why so many people in the public eye are suspicious of the press. Ever since that incident, I've tried hard to play a straight bat to reporters and keep my own personal thoughts to myself.

The truth is, however you want to choose the words, some of my players were 'not brave'. When I asked for volunteers, our designated penalty-takers looked the other way. Two or three other senior players stared at their boots and stayed silent. If I had been the manager of Germany or the USA, 11 hands would have immediately gone up and they would have been arguing with one another as to why each of them had the right to take a penalty.

If you want to make the leap from being a good player in a good side to joining the very best in the world, as a player, as an individual, you must have the bottle to put your hand up in pressure situations like these. I set the highest possible standards for my squads, because I believed they were capable of going that extra mile to compete with the very best. So, yes, I was disappointed that some of my players shirked it and looked the other way. Later when we got back to our hotel, four or five of the girls looked somewhat sheepish.

At our next meeting, I told the players the context of how my remarks had got into the press. I told them to deal with it and move on. Some of them may have been narked by the accusation, but in their hearts they know they should have put their hands up and taken responsibility for the good of the team. They should have been braver. Because at the top level of sport, it is only the fearless who succeed. To be honest, with a semi-final place at stake, and then possibly a final, their reluctance shocked me at the time.

But, in hindsight, perhaps not.

There is, I believe, a mentality problem in English football – not just with the women, but the men too. You can put systems in place to ensure your players are among the fittest, strongest and most athletic in the world. You can work endlessly with them on their individual physical strengths and weaknesses, develop their talents and tactical thinking. You can work with sports psychologists to develop players' confidence. All of these things can help contribute towards creating a winning mentality.

But, in the end, players have to take responsibility for themselves. I completely understand that fear of failure can cripple some players thoughts. But they are, almost without exception, the players who will never make it to the very top. If England players – both men and women – want to win World Cups and European Championships – again and again, like the Germans, the Brazilians, the Americans – then it's down to individual players working on their own mentality and taking more responsibility for themselves.

Despite all her demons and vulnerabilities, on a football pitch Kelly Smith was an England player who had a totally winning mentality. Whether or not all her playing experience in the USA had a bearing on that, I don't know, but the Americans only ever expect to win. Their mentality is like the Germans'.

I was roundly condemned for describing some of my players' reluctance to step forward as cowardice. Well, you know what, players have to hear the truth from their managers, and sometimes it hurts. It was just a shame the manner in which they heard it was totally out of context.

In the *Telegraph*, former rugby player Brian Moore criticised me for not making my players practise taking penalties before the game and for not having a pre-arranged running order of penalty-takers. If he had done his research, Brian would have discovered that we practised penalties endlessly. Everyone has their opinion, and coaches and managers in both the men's and women's games have different ways of approaching penalty-taking. Pretty much every international player already has the technique and ability to score penalties. Some managers say that you can practise them in training until the cows come home. But that would never replicate the big-match atmosphere experience of a penalty shoot-out. In the end, it's all about confidence and dealing with a high-pressure situation. I can understand those thoughts but, being meticulous in my preparations, I always made sure that all of my players practised penalty-taking in training. They were technically prepared as much as they could have been.

So it doesn't help group confidence when players are looking the other way and not volunteering. The French contingent could all see what was happening, and a group of my players handed them a psychological edge going into the shoot-out. To this day, I have immense admiration for Claire Rafferty, a raw debutante, who could rightly have hidden behind the more experienced players. But she was the first to volunteer.

In the end, although I was very disappointed in some of my players, the whole thing was blown out of proportion. I told the squad (and the press) that, that incident aside, I was incredibly proud of them for how they'd performed throughout the tournament. But my remarks about the lack of volunteers for the penalty-taking were the ones that gained all the headlines.

What was really frustrating was not winning. But we ended the tournament unbeaten in normal time, and we'd all learnt a lot more about big-match pressure situations. And thanks to our performances, we'd risen to sixth in the FIFA world rankings.

What I learnt personally was that with increased media coverage comes much greater scrutiny – and if you lose, greater criticism. I couldn't really complain about that because, for years, I'd been working hard to get more visibility for the women's game. I certainly don't think it's true that all publicity is good publicity, but you have to be prepared to take the rough with the smooth when you're in the public eye.

Chapter 16

London 2012

I wanted nothing to do with managing the Great Britain Olympic team.

In 2011, we were at the World Cup. I was trying to get us to qualify for the 2013 Euros. Plus there was the small matter of still being in charge of the five levels in the pyramid underneath the senior team from under-15s to under-23s. I still oversaw the coach- and scout-mentoring schemes and the FA's National Development Centre at Loughborough University. I don't think people realised just how much work that involved. My days all started early and generally finished very late. There weren't many genuine days off and, every day, I had to wear a number of different hats. By and large, I have a lot of drive and energy. But I thought there was just too much on my plate to take on the extra responsibility of heading up the Olympic team. I was asked and turned the job down. And that should have been the end of the story.

But Pippa and Pav kept working on me. Michelle said I was an idiot to turn it down. My old friend Stuart Pearce had said 'yes' to the men's job, and the idea of working alongside him certainly appealed. The powers that be asked me again and I reconsidered. In the end, I had to eat humble pie and say I had been wrong to turn it down in the first place. Because managing the GB team turned out to be one of the greatest, most joyful experiences of my life.

It was the first time that women's football had ever featured in the Olympics and there was a lot of behind-the-scenes work I had to do before even choosing the squad. Because it was GB, I had to liaise with the heads of the Scottish, Welsh and Northern Ireland FAs to get their co-operation. I went to stacks of meetings and, initially, they were rather like diplomatic missions. At first, the Northern Irish were reluctant to become involved, but were eventually co-operative. Scotland's manager Anna Signeul was a real help and support. But the Welsh FA and their Finnish manager, Jarmo Matikainen, just didn't want to know. I had all the home nations players extensively scouted before I chose the squad, Wales included. I sent Alan May over to the Cyprus Cup to watch the Welsh in action and talk to Jarmo. Alan asked him who he regarded as his best players. Jarmo just shrugged and said, 'All of them.'

There is, of course, a history to this. All the home nations, particularly the smaller ones, have been wary of being part of a GB football team. Their understandable concern is that FIFA and UEFA might take international status away from them. No more Scotland, Wales or Northern Ireland. I also suspected that they were wary of the FA taking all the power and decision-making away from them.

Eight years previously the Olympic Committee had turned down an application for GB men's and women's teams to play at the 2008 Beijing Olympics because the squads would be made up of players from different Football Associations. So this time around, we'd been honoured that the IOC helped to mark the Olympics in

London by finally granting permission for this. Northern Ireland, Wales and Scotland didn't quite see it that way. But I was tasked with putting together a GB team and that's what I did.

It was a tough job picking the final 18 and, as it turned out, 16 of them were my England players. No Welsh or Irish, and just two players from the Scotland team, Kim Little and Ifeoma Dieke. A lot of people didn't like that. But I was asked to pick the best squad of players available to play. We had everyone looked at extensively and, I think for me, I took the country associations out of the equation.

We prepared for the tournament by playing a behind-the-scenes training match against South Africa in Birmingham. Then it was up to Middlesbrough, alongside Stuart and his squad, for a few days of training, plus a full friendly against Sweden at the Riverside. We all went up on the train together. Though we didn't share training, we were in the same hotel and training complex, eating and relaxing together. There was a great atmosphere in the joint camp and the GB guys were a pleasure to be around. It was rare that men and women's squads hung out together. The two camps played pool, talked football and got along famously. I did, though, have to clip one of the England lads around the back of the head one evening when he was ogling a couple of the girls: 'Keep your eyes off my players!'

We drew 0–0 against Sweden and, as ever, there were important lessons to learn from our performance. It was good to talk football again with Stuart, too. We'd first become friends when we did our pro licences together years before, and when he was appointed England under-21 boss we became partners in crime together at the FA. We helped keep one another sane through the endless meetings that were often the order of the day at Soho Square.

Though both of us were hardly 'committee people', we soon learnt that if we were going to get what we wanted, we'd have to learn how to play the game.

I always trusted Stuart – and still do – because he's always honest. I think we're quite similar – we don't suffer fools gladly and try to be straight with people about what we believe in. Some people don't like that, but, well … tough. And, like me, he's always up front about the fact that he's always learning. I like Stuart a lot – and I respect him a great deal.

Although our first group game was in Cardiff at the Millennium Stadium, I felt it was important for the players to get the full-on London 2012 experience by spending a couple of nights in the Olympic village before we travelled to Wales. I'm so glad we did, because it was amazing rubbing shoulders with the likes of Usain Bolt, Mo Farah, and competitors from all over the world contesting dozens of different sports. We'd all go down to the gyms and training areas and get a fantastic insight into how different sportsmen and women prepared themselves. There was such intensity of purpose and, as a coach, so many things to take on board and learn from all of the different disciplines, and different shapes of people from different cultures and sports.

There was a 24-hour food hall where you could get any style of cuisine from anywhere around the world. Astonishingly, it could hold 5,000 diners. We had the opportunity to chat with every culture, every ethnicity. It was a wonderful melting pot, full of ambitious people from all corners of the earth who were there to compete and win, but also to make friends and share in the moment. In so many ways, the Olympic village showed you exactly what was great, what was best about people the world over. It gave the players a massive lift to mix with all these top sportsmen and women. So before we travelled to Cardiff, I decided to draft someone in who would hopefully be the cream on the cake. Someone I knew who would really inspire them in their journey into the group matches – Dame Kelly Holmes.

She was really happy to come in to talk to the players, and was truly motivating. I think what really hit home with the squad was when she told them, 'Now you are no longer just footballers. Now you are Olympians.' You could sense the hairs going up on the backs of everyone's necks. There was a slight intake of breath, as everyone privately understood exactly what she meant.

The Olympic village was an incredible bubble. Like me, quite a few sportsmen and women came from the London area. But it felt like we were all somewhere very different. My home in Nunhead was only a few miles away, but it felt like I was a thousand miles away. As a Londoner, I knew Stratford well. Up until the building work had started, the site of the Olympic village was a bit of a wasteland. Now it was a gorgeous park full of world-class sporting facilities. I felt sad for all the people who wanted to knock it and be negative.

The 2012 Olympics really were special outside of London, too. We went to our base in Wales where we were to be the very first event in the Games, two days before the actual opening ceremony. It was such an honour for women's football. Of all the amazing sports and sports people that would feature in the Olympics, we were chosen to be the trailblazers, the athletes who would light the blue touch paper for the greatest sports event ever to happen in Great Britain. GB v New Zealand would be the very first match. Our group also contained Marta's Brazil and the unpredictable Cameroonians. So a good start was vital.

My starting line up against New Zealand was Karen Bardsley, Alex Scott, Jill Scott, Ifeoma Dieke, Steph Houghton, Karen Carney, Casey Stoney, Kim Little, Anita Asante, Kelly Smith and Eni Aluko. Selecting a GB team allowed me the opportunity to pick two really exciting Scots players in Kim Little and Ifeoma Dieke. There was nothing political about it. I'd watched them both and had them thoroughly scouted. Kim had real quality and a low centre of gravity. Her movement was high-end stuff. Ife had impressed in training, too. She had pace and was physically very strong. I was keen to see how they would fit in with the rest of my England players.

The Millennium Stadium in Cardiff is a spectacular sporting venue at the best of times. But packed with 40,000 noisy, raucous fans – the great majority supporting GB – the atmosphere was electric. There was a real sense that the seven years of waiting, since winning the bid, were now over. Sepp Blatter and Sebastian Coe – then FIFA president and chairman of the 2012 Olympic organising committee respectively – were in the stands. My God, it was happening. The Olympics were here.

It was a sweltering hot summer's afternoon, and all I could smell as I sat down in the coaching area was suntan cream. It was wonderful to see how many children and families were together in the stands, so many of them dressed in GB t-shirts and hats, faces painted in red, white and blue. In such a highly charged atmosphere, it was perhaps understandable that we made a nervy start. We increasingly took control, but didn't come near to scoring until late in the first half, when Anita Asante got on the end of an Eni Aluko cross and hit the post. In the second half, Kelly Smith put Ellen White clean through with a pinpoint pass. But with only the goalie to beat, Ellen stalled and the ball was cleared. A minute later came our moment of glory. We got a free-kick on the edge of the box. Calm as you like, Steph Houghton stepped up and buried the ball into the corner with her right foot. We played it out to win our first group game 1–0. It wasn't the greatest game of football anyone would ever see, but it was a wonderful spectacle.

I asked the girls to take a lap of honour. Not so much to gain applause for themselves, although they deserved it, but to applaud the wonderful crowd who'd roared on their every touch of the ball. I told the players afterwards that they had made history. This match would live long in the memory, not for the football but certainly for the sense of occasion.

I was exhilarated and stayed on at the stadium with some of my staff to scout the second game from our group, Cameroon v Brazil. The Brazilians were irresistible and hammered the Cameroonians 5–0. I decided rather than take a car down to the hotel, I'd walk the ten minutes back from the Millennium. I told security and initially Yvonne wasn't keen. I pooh-poohed it, but soon realised why she had misgivings. She'd gauged the situation far better than I had. Pippa, Rachel Pav, Keith Rees, Brent and a group of others decided to join me. We stepped out of the stadium and I was absolutely mobbed. Believe me, this is not a normal occurrence. But there were dozens of kids and their parents and fans in general who utterly besieged us in the street. I very happily spent nearly an hour signing autographs, chatting to fans and posing for photographs with people. It really struck me then that this Olympics was going to be something very special indeed. And that it would really help push the profile of women's football in this country.

With three points already on the board, we took on Cameroon in our second group match. They were a tough, hard-tackling outfit who also had flair. They were sometimes inspirational, sometimes not. Brazil had hammered them, but the Cameroons could never be taken for granted. Though I'd done all the preparation I could, we were never quite sure which Cameroon would turn up on the day.

Earlier that day Brazil had narrowly beaten New Zealand 1–0. So we knew that a win against the Cameroons would qualify us with a game to spare. And as that spare game was against Brazil, we were keen to get three points.

For a lot of the first half they kicked bits out of us. But this led to a free-kick after Kelly Smith had been hacked to the floor. The Cameroon defence failed to deal with it, and Casey Stoney stabbed home from close range. The second goal was a stunner. Kim Little picked up a perfectly timed pass from Kelly Smith and then clipped the ball into the path of Jill Scott. Imperiously, she made room for herself and then hammered it past the Cameroon goalie. We went in at half-time a comfortable 2–0 up. At the start of the second half, Cameroon realised it was shit or bust: lose to us, and they were out. So they came back at us with real aggression. We stayed calm and, ten minutes before the end of the game, put it beyond doubt. Kim Little was once again the provider, putting Steph Houghton through to strike home from the edge of the area. Two goals in two games: not a bad return for a defender. Six points to the good, we were through to the quarter-finals. But could we beat Brazil and top the group? For this game, we would travel from Cardiff and play at Wembley, the world home of football. It was likely that whoever got the best of this one would be group winners and avoid world champions Japan in the last eight.

The Brazil game was a remarkable occasion for women's football in Britain. As we were settling into our dressing room, a friend sent a photo to my phone. It was Wembley Way absolutely packed with thousands of fans on their way into the match. Now let's get this into perspective. As a player and as a manager, I've been involved in England games in the past that played out in front of a few hundred fans. This was something big. Like a major breakthrough was happening for women's football.

The players got to meet so many dignitaries I think they combed their hair about a thousand times. They were absolutely made up. David Beckham had sent me a few e-mails with good wishes, which I passed on to the girls, although I'm not sure they believed me.

Before the game, the Brazilian manager Jorge Barcellos was so friendly, so generous of spirit – but he also exuded a sense of superiority. No way did he expect Brazil to come away from this match with anything but a win – I could absolutely see it in his eyes. He had Cristiane, the leading goalscorer in World Cup history, alongside numerous world-class players as his squad. He also had Marta.

If women's football has ever had a Pelé then it is Marta. At the time of this book going to press, she'd scored 92 goals in 95 Brazil matches; back then she'd been named FIFA World Player of the Year five times in a row between 2006 and 2010. In the 2007 World Cup she won both the Golden Ball award as best player and the Golden Boot award as top scorer.

It's hard to explain what happens to a manager during a game. The tunnel vision you get. As I came out with the players and then made my way to the bench, I was so in the zone with myself – talking to my assistants, thinking over decisions I'd made about tactics, thoughts about individual players, how to change tack if the game was going against us – that I was largely unaware of 70,000 people cheering and chanting, or the National Anthem being played. It's only when I watched it afterwards that I realised what had been happening around me.

We made an electric start, scoring after two minutes. Karen Carney twisted free of the Brazilian defence over on the right and sent over a low cross which Steph Houghton reached before Brazil's goalie Andréia, and forced home past her marker from a wickedly tight angle.

On 25 minutes, my heart skipped a beat when Alex Scott headed the ball against her own post, under pressure from a Brazilian attacker, but luck was on our side as it bounced straight back out. Then in the second half, we nearly went 2–0 up when Eniola Aluko got legged over by Francielle. Penalty! But Kelly, who'd come back from months and months of injury problems, put it too close to Andréia, who saved it easily. I was gutted for Kelly: she'd fought so hard to get match fit for the Games and she deserved a break. But we held on.

It wasn't the best we'd ever played during my time as manager – France in the qualifiers, Germany in 2007; those were two terrific performances – but as an occasion, the Brazil game was something else. The crowd and the atmosphere gave our players an extra ten per cent. After the whistle, Jorge Barcellos had gone from being smiley-faced to pretty damned sullen. I said, 'You have to give me a hug,' and kept beckoning him towards me.

We topped group E, Brazil came second, which meant that they drew the world champions Japan in the quarter-finals, while we played the theoretically much more beatable Canada – 'theoretically', as they were ranked seventh in the world at the time. So much for theory.

The girls had put so much physical and emotional energy into the Brazil match that when the Canada game came around some of them were a bit leggy and mentally drained. But that's where the excuses end. Canada deserved to win. They scored twice in the first 25 minutes and no matter what we tried to throw at them, they showed a great deal of professionalism in closing us out of the game. Crazy though this may sound, one of my enduring memories of that game is of a fan just behind the coaching area who kept screaming at me for most of the second half. 'Hope! Hope! You've got to do something!' At the time, it alternately annoyed and amused me, this flea constantly in my ear. But, in hindsight, it was progress: fans were getting so hyper and so involved with us as a team. So, whoever you were, thank you.

And so we went out. Though I would have loved for us to get a podium finish, London 2012 was an unbelievable experience for everyone. I was proud of my players, and all the telling contributions my staff had put in. I loved the Olympics and feel privileged to have been a part of it all.

Chapter 17

2013

The London Olympics was such an amazing experience for everyone, I knew my next big task was to ensure the players didn't regard the qualifying games for the 2013 Euros as all a bit after the Lord Mayor's show. I needn't have worried. We put in a string of thoroughly professional performances, home and away, against the Netherlands, Serbia, Croatia and Slovenia, and ended up as unbeaten group 6 winners. We won six matches, including a 6–0 away victory in Croatia and a 4–0 away win in Slovenia. The most pleasing thing for me was our goal difference. We scored 22 goals and conceded just two – and those were both in the same game, a 2–2 draw in Serbia. So, there were seven clean sheets, including a 0–0 away draw against the Netherlands. And I hadn't lost a qualifying match in ten years.

All the years I'd worked on our defending, trying to make us at the very least hard to beat, seemed to be working. As usual, we had injuries to a number of players I'd like to have picked for the squad, but at the end of the day, we now had a lot of strength in depth. My 23 players were Karen Bardsley, Rachel Brown-Finnis and Siobhan Chamberlain in goal; defenders Anita Asante, Laura Bassett, Gemma Bonner, Sophie Bradley, Lucy Bronze, Steph Houghton, Alex Scott, Dunia Susi and Casey Stoney; midfielders

Eni Aluko, Karen Carney, Jess Clarke, Jade Moore, Jordan Nobbs, Jill Scott, Fara Williams and Rachel Yankey; and forwards Kelly Smith, Toni Duggan, and Ellen White.

We went to Sweden for the Euro finals in good spirits and with high hopes. The BBC was broadcasting all our games live and we'd been getting a lot of press and media coverage back home. Sweden had embraced the tournament with gusto, and our base in Linköping was buzzing ahead of our group games there. A city of 150,000 people in southern Sweden, Linköping liked its sport. There were shops and market stalls all over the city selling England shirts and souvenirs, and a lot of English fans had come out to watch us. Linköping even had its own fan zone in the town square. A lot of the locals were supporting England in the group games, and partly because our defender Anita Asante was playing in Sweden at the time for Göteborg.

We had great training facilities, a good hotel and preparations appeared to have gone well. We came into the opening group game against Spain ranked 11 places above them in the world rankings. But they were a good side, having beaten world champions Germany in their qualifiers.

It was a topsy-turvy start. After only three minutes, we were behind to a Verónica Boquete strike. Three minutes later Eni Aluko pounced on a through ball from Jill Scott and fired it into the bottom left-hand corner. The rest of the first half was end to end, but our touch was off, there were too many unforced errors. We looked a little nervy in possession. I was fairly glad to get us in at half-time at one each.

In the second half, both sides largely cancelled one another out until five minutes of madness at the end of the game. A poor clearance out of defence found Jennifer Hermoso inside the box.

And although we had Karen Bardsley and four defenders on the line, the Spaniard rifled it into the net to make it 2–1 to Spain. But heads didn't drop, and a minute later Laura Bassett swung at a Rachel Yankey corner and we were back level.

I would have been more than happy with the draw, given the circumstances, but there was more almost comic drama to come. In stoppage time, Spanish substitute Alexia Putellas fired over a corner, which Karen Bardsley seemed to get two hands on. But the Spanish challenged her very aggressively and the ball bounced into the net off the back of her head. But, in truth, in a different game, it could just easily have been given as a free-kick. Spain were ahead again, but this time there was no way back. The whistle blew and we had lost 3–2.

Losing after coming back from behind twice was hard to take. The players were very edgy, particularly in the first half, and I think they were really feeling the increased sense of expectation. Our touch was off, there were too many unenforced errors. They fought hard to pull back from 1–0 and then 2–1 but, in the end, a bizarre mistake lost us the game.

For the Russia game in Linköping, I decided to field an unchanged side. Alex Scott won her 100th cap so I made her captain for the match. On two minutes, Karen Bardsley did really well to take a dangerous early cross from Elena Terekhova. Two minutes later she dived to her right to save a well-directed header from Olga Petrova. After a poor display against Spain, this was the kind of start which would have done her confidence a power of good.

We were looking much more lively but, after 15 minutes, disaster struck. Rachel Yankey pulled up sharply with a hamstring problem, and had to be replaced by Karen Carney. The longer we searched for the opener, the more lacklustre we became. We created plenty of chances, but composure in front of goal was in short supply. Seven minutes before the break, and just as we'd done against Spain, we got sloppy. Elena Morozova sent in a deep cross from the left, and it caught out our backline completely. Terekhova nipped in, said, 'Thank you very much,' and tapped it home from close range. We went in at half-time 1–0 down.

Throughout the second half, we continued to press but there was no great urgency to the performance. Kelly Smith came on and immediately injected some drive into the side. We hit the woodwork a couple of times, but the Russians rode their luck and defended with real purpose. The minutes were racing by like seconds now, and we were into injury time. I exhorted the players forward and, just when it looked like we would be going home, super subs Toni Duggan and Kelly Smith combined to score a last-gasp equaliser. Kelly flighted the ball across the area, Toni controlled it with one touch and fired it low past Elvira Todua from ten yards out.

I was happy for the players. We were looking to get three points from Russia to help us progress but, under the circumstances, a point was welcome. Although once again I was mystified by our performance. We had sparked then spluttered, gone on and off the boil and generally played without any great level of consistency.

As a manager, you can shout and bawl from the touchline, ask and demand that the players change shape, move the ball quicker, whatever. As a former international player, you want to be out there on the pitch to help make some difference and give some new drive to the performance. But, of course, you can't, and that is what's so frustrating. It was a crazy game. We dominated it, but conceded a sloppy goal. In patches we were so slow at coming out, a bit deliberate, we just didn't shift the ball quickly enough.

The reality now was that we had to beat France to qualify for the last eight knockout round. We'd made progress by drawing our last two matches against them, but we had never beaten the French in tournament football. In the build-up to the game, I told the players it was do or die. This had to be England on their A-game for 90 minutes plus.

From the whistle, the French came at us with searing pace. A Le Sommer screamer hit the post after eight minutes; a minute later she controlled the ball on the edge of the penalty area and shot into the bottom corner to make it 1–0. It was only thanks to some Karen Bardsley heroics that we didn't go further behind in the first half. She made two last-gasp saves to deny Élodie Thomis and Louisa Nécib and pretty much kept us in the game. I couldn't fault our players for effort, but France's quicker passing and constant threat in the final third kept us firmly pinned back and, throughout the first half, we didn't manage one single shot on target.

It was a measure of the control France had in the game that our first chance on goal came after an hour, a shot from Toni Duggan. But this encouragement was short-lived. Two goals in three minutes ended any hopes we had of getting back into the game, with a clever Nécib finish followed by a Wendie Renard header. In all honesty, the French were irresistible – in the end we were outclassed. We were out at the group stages and were under the spotlight like never before – unfortunately we wilted.

It was a bitterly disappointing end to the tournament. I don't want to sound glib, but the awkward thing about World and European Cups is that a lot of other good teams want to win them as well. We caught the French on a day when they were on fire – and, once again, we just weren't firing at all.

I prepared myself for the inevitable journalistic post-mortem in the press conference after the match. Things can get very black and white with the English sporting press. You're either a hero or a zero. After the France game, I knew the questioning would portray me pretty much as a zero. Fair enough, we'd got knocked out at the group stage and so much more was expected of us. I expected so much more. But the press conference really made me laugh. 'What now Hope? Are you thinking of resigning?' 'Why did we play so poorly?' The line of questioning made it feel like we'd set out to lose. I was desperately disappointed that we didn't make better progress or show ourselves at our best. But it was like the end of the world had happened. This was the fifth major tournament in a row that we'd appeared in. Though they had underperformed, this was a strong squad of players who were developing and progressing. Of course 2013 was a step backwards, but that happens in football. The important thing was how we would bounce back from the disappointment.

As I said at the time, we played better against France than in the first two games in the group. We came out of the blocks and really had a go. It was a gallant effort right up to the end, but unfortunately it was never enough. A lot of credit to France: a very good team in all departments, and they were just too much for us.

We struggled in that tournament, we just didn't click. We put in some brave efforts, but weren't good enough. I'm not going to make excuses. We had injuries in the build-up, but I feel we picked our best players available. I'm very proud of the players, proud of the staff. We came with the best intentions, but we had to accept we weren't quite good enough on the day.

Even in hindsight, it's hard to put my finger on exactly what went wrong. Of course, like anything it probably involved a number of different factors. Without a doubt, the players underperformed. I know that some were managing injuries, which I was criticised for. But, in truth, there are certain footballers – like Kelly Smith, Casey Stoney and Rachel Yankey, for example – who, despite any temporary losses of form, are just such big tournament players, you're prepared to take a gamble on them. Not in a foolhardy way – as I've outlined, I would always take advice from Pippa and her team. If they had said any of those players were too much of a gamble, I wouldn't have picked them in the squad.

In previous tournaments, Kelly had come into matches carrying injuries – but had then gone on to score crucial goals for us. Faye White had often struggled with injuries coming into tournaments and sometimes during them, but still continued to give a string of player-of-the-match performances. We had come into Euro 2013 missing a few key performers through injury, like Anita Asante and Claire Rafferty but, again, that was no excuse. We had depth in our squad. As usual, the preparations were spot on in terms of the opposition, the camp we had. We prepared meticulously for the tournament. Little was left to chance in any department, and there was nothing that we did differently from the previous few tournaments. Once again, I couldn't fault my back-up staff, who worked round the clock in Sweden to support the squad.

How much was I to blame? I've always been absolutely clear that, as manager, the buck stops with me. Being honest, I came into the tournament feeling bloody tired. Rather like my experience in front of the mirror in Wolfsburg, I was feeling drained from the many number of hats I was forced to wear as manager of the whole women's system. Though the previous two years had been exciting – the 2011 World Cup, 2012 Olympics, planning for qualifiers to get us to Canada in 2015, helping with the Women's Super League and all my usual duties – it was exhausting too. Maybe my tiredness had something to do with it? Perhaps I didn't have the spark or energy to enthuse the players more than they needed?

To my knowledge, there wasn't any particular unrest among the players, certainly no revolt against what we were trying to do. Players always complain and moan about their managers among themselves – I know I did. I'm sure I wasn't particularly popular with some of my players, and certainly those who weren't being picked in the starting 11. But you're not there to be chummy chums with your players. You have to make hard decisions. And in terms of what we were trying to achieve out on the training ground, and on the pitch, everyone seemed happy to move in the same direction. They were just fed up with their performances and their results and, believe me, a losing camp can never be a truly happy one. The players were hardly turning cartwheels as one poor result came after another.

Something was different about this tournament. The 2012 Olympics had been quite the media circus, but the girls had, by and large, all managed to remain focused on their football. The 2013 Euros offered too many distractions for the players. It was wonderful that we were getting such wide coverage on TV, radio, internet and in the press, but it was starting to have an effect on some of the girls.

In the main, the squad loved being in the spotlight, and why not? It's good for players to have some distractions during tournaments, but after a while in Sweden it became silly. The press and media were in our hotel throughout the build-up and the group games, and it was one interview or stunt after another. We had agreed designated press conference and press interview times with the media, but increasingly the girls were being asked to take part in press stunts outside of those times, and I think some of the players were allowing their heads to be turned a little by all the media attention. For years, I'd been battling to get more publicity and coverage for women's football in England, but what Sweden taught me was that you need to be careful in what you wish for. Yes, like most football managers, I am a control freak. You want to try to control and anticipate everything you can to keep your players focused on the task ahead. When the media circus moves in, that focus can dissipate. At times, I felt that the atmosphere in the camp was being controlled more by outside influences that were not about football. Some of the players had long discussions about what colour boots to wear. In the minutes before the Russia game kicked off, some of the girls seemed more concerned about whether their shoelaces matched their headbands, because the match was being televised to a big global audience.

I offer these thoughts not as excuses from me for our poor performances, but as observations over the many possible reasons why things didn't turn out differently. I was the manager and take total responsibility for our poor showing in Sweden. My hope was that I could go away and sit down with my staff and piece together what we needed to learn from the tournament, so that we could move forward again.

I should have guessed that something was afoot when I returned to Sweden a week or so later to watch Germany beat the hosts 1–0 in the Euro final. General secretary Alex Horne was there in the stadium, along with a few others from the FA. Nobody I talked to said a word about us getting knocked out. Everyone was keeping schtum. You just know when people are skirting around an issue and not mentioning the elephant in the room that something's afoot.

Back at the FA, I waited for my bosses to call a meeting so that we could debrief on the Euros, but it never came. So I asked for a meeting to be held. The date was set for 8 August 2013, which would become a day I will never forget.

Prior to the meeting, I'd started to get slightly unnerved about just how silent the Club England suits continued to be about the Euros. Whenever the subject was brought up, it would be quickly changed. I'd been round the block enough times to know that something was wrong, so I talked to a solicitor friend of mine, Kehinde Adeogun. She advised me to ask in advance what would be on the agenda for the meeting. I did and it was brief and to the point – one item and one item only, 'debrief of European Championships', which was an oddly short agenda. My friend advised me to go in and take notes or even record the meeting. I also decided to ask Michelle to come in with me as moral and emotional support. Not in the meeting itself, but to accompany me to Wembley.

Though I already had my doubts about whether or not we would be actually debriefing on the Euros, I put together a file of stats, facts and opinions about why I thought we had failed – broadly explaining what I've already outlined. I dressed smartly and we drove in to the FA's Wembley HQ. I went in for my meeting, while Michelle waited in the car. The moment I arrived, I was ushered into an office where just two people were sat behind the desk, head of Club England Adrian Bevington and

Alex Horne. No one else. No Trevor Brooking, even though he was my line manager.

Adrian came straight to the point: 'Hope, we're going to have to let you go.'

It took a while to sink in. No, we hadn't performed well at the Euros, and that's why we did actually need a debrief – to work out why and put it right. For 15 years, I had been told by the FA that my contract as England manager – and in charge of the pyramid underneath it – was most definitely not results orientated. In those 15 years, we had made much progress from grassroots level up.

I said, 'Really? Why is that then?'

I'm not sure they were expecting that. Adrian said, 'Well, the results didn't go well in the Euros.'

I replied, 'I didn't know I had a contract that was results led.'

Alex Horne didn't say a word. So I asked him, 'Alex, aren't you going to say anything?'

He mumbled something about poor results, too.

Adrian said to me, 'Thank you for everything you've done.'

I shrugged and said, 'It doesn't really feel like I'm being thanked.'

Who wants to be sacked for doing a good job right across the board?

I very pointedly asked Adrian where Trevor Brooking was. He was after all, my line manager. Adrian said he 'had to be somewhere'. I'd worked at the FA for 15 years and now I was being sacked. But Trevor Brooking couldn't be there.

They asked me not to pass on the news until it had been officially announced, and then brought up the gagging order. In return for a pay-off, I would have to agree not to talk publically about my sacking, the FA, or comment upon my time in the building. They talked a little about how I would be paid off and urged me to visit the people in HR to discuss it. But I'd had enough. I got up and left the FA offices for the very last time.

I told Michelle and she was devastated, in tears. But I needed to stay focused. Kehinde had advised me to take detailed notes, so once we got home I told Michelle what had been discussed and she wrote it all down. Then I rang two of the people closest to me, in confidence, to offload about what had happened. I rang Rachel Pav and she was so upset she just burst into tears. I spoke to Alan and he was stunned. All I could remember from the phone call was long silences from his end – and Alan was never lost for words.

Then I spoke to the League Managers Association and they were brilliant. They told me to switch off my mobile and to stay schtum until further notice. If anyone from the FA contacted me, I was to immediately refer them to the LMA without any comment. It was a huge relief to have them on my side. The LMA did everything for me, sorting out all the financial and legal aspects of my sacking. It took a lot of pressure off. It made me smile. A few years before, Howard Wilkinson had virtually ordered me to join the LMA. I didn't really understand at the time why it was so important to be a member, but I did now. And the irony was that in 2013 the LMA's chairman was none other than Howard. It felt like he'd come back to help me yet again.

I had already agreed to be a technical observer for UEFA at an international under-19 tournament in Wales and didn't want to go back on my word, so I travelled west with Michelle, hoping that immersing myself in some football would take my mind off what had happened. I couldn't have been more wrong. Everywhere I went, I was introduced as England manager Hope Powell. Coaches and players asked me what my plans were for the World Cup qualifiers. Was I looking at any new caps? Would I make many changes? It was excruciatingly difficult, because I couldn't tell anybody what had happened. I was pretending that I was still England manager. I was living a lie, and I couldn't do that. So I went to the tournament organisers and told them in confidence about how awkward and compromised I was feeling. I asked if they would mind if I left and went home to London, because I also knew that once the official announcement was made, there would be a media storm around the tournament. The attention would be on me, and not the under-19s, and that wouldn't have been fair. The UEFA officials were great about it, but were also incredibly surprised that I'd been given the sack. Not for the last time, the general feeling was also one of shock that I hadn't been found any other role within the FA.

It had been hinted at and speculated over for a couple of years that the FA were considering the creation of a new post – a head of Women's Football. My name was continually linked with it in the press and, in truth, if it had been offered to me, I would have accepted. But Trevor Brooking and I had very different ideas about what such a role would involve. I believed the post should be one of technical director, responsible for women's football all the way through the age levels from under-15s to the senior squad. Underneath the technical director, a head coach or manager would take charge of the teams at each of the levels. Trevor had other ideas. He wanted it to be a post that was only responsible for the under-19s down and based at the FA's new St George's centre. I said to him, 'So, if I was to apply, it would not be a promotion?' He shrugged and, in doing so, in the most roundabout of ways, made me instinctively realise that I wouldn't be in the running for the job anyway.

In the end, they reorganised things so that Brent was made head of Elite Development, Women's Football. Kelly Simmons was put in charge of grassroots and the Women's Super League, Mark Sampson was, of course, made England team manager. It makes me laugh. Even before you take into consideration all the other responsibilities I had at the FA, they now pretty much have three people doing my old job.

It now seems obvious that the poor performances in Sweden gave the FA the excuse they needed to get rid of me completely.

Recently, I attended the Champions League final in Berlin 2014, as one of the technical observers for UEFA. There, I met up with my old friend Silvia Neid. A month or so beforehand, the German FA had announced that Silvia was retiring as national head coach in 2016, to be replaced by Steffi Jones. I asked her why she was quitting now. Silvia smiled and told me she wanted to improve her golf handicap. But, more seriously, wanted more time with her family, her friends – and her life. I could absolutely relate to that and the pressure on Silvia to keep delivering trophies must have been immense.

But the big difference between Silvia and I was that the German FA were so keen not to waste all her years of experience, they made her the new head of their scouting department and handed her a contract that lasted for years.

On 16 August 2013, the FA made the official announcement about my sacking, which I must say was a great relief. It contained all the standard empty corporate platitudes, but at least it was now public and I could start to move forward.

There was a deafening silence from some of my former players, which is to be expected when any manager gets the sack. They're understandably looking forward to trying to get selected by their new boss and don't want to stick up for the old regime. I'm realistic enough to know that there were a number of players who didn't like my style and were glad to see the back of me. Anyone who's a manager who wants to be liked is on to a loser. It is most definitely not a popularity contest. That's football. It will be very interesting to talk in the future to some of my players who make it into management. They'll soon get a very different perspective on the tough decisions managers have to make and the flak they'll receive from players as a consequence.

Some of the players sent me very kind texts. One player, though, was very public about my sacking, and I want to quote Casey Stoney's comments to the BBC because I felt it was a very thoughtful analysis of the situation:

Hope was not afraid to make decisions that upset people. She did what she thought was right. It can't have been that wrong because she reached a European final and two World Cup quarter-finals. She was ruthless.

I can't thank Hope enough for the opportunity she has given me. She's made my dreams come true by giving me the chance to play for England and making me captain.

She took the England job to a whole new level and maybe the FA now thinks it's time to go the next level. There was unrest (in the England camp at the Euros) but that came because we were losing games. If you are winning matches, then nobody is going to ask questions, are they? Unfortunately, the buck stops with the manager when you underperform.

But you can't forget what Hope has done for women's football in the last 15 years. It's a long time and I'm sure she will look back and reflect and be massively proud. She has changed the structure of the game from grassroots upwards, the player pathways … she and [FA national game director] Kelly Simmons have worked very hard together to change the women's game.

It was typical of Casey that she spoke up honestly. She has always taken responsibility for herself and her opinions. Casey's right – I was ruthless, because I had to be. If I was a bit of a sergeant major it was for good reason. There was so much that had to be developed and changed when I first took over and it was vital that I was tough and single-minded. Being a push-over or a 'yes girl' would not have helped the women's game one iota.

There are people within the FA who are extremely conservative and don't like change. More importantly, there are men there who don't 'get' women's football or why it's so important to develop. I don't want to name names because I don't want this book to be about personal score settling – and in many ways the names don't matter. They can only look to themselves as to why equal opportunities shouldn't be actively fought for on behalf of their own daughters, wives, sisters or girlfriends. I will always continue to fight for equality of opportunity regardless of gender, race or sexuality.

When you're working class and black, never mind having a same-sex partner, you learn early on in life that you're going to have to fight for everything you achieve. I got used to that from an early age; it's the hand that life has dealt. Along the way you also soon realise that a lot of the work you try to do will be faced with ignorance and fear. You will come up against people who have a total sense of entitlement and privilege. They pretty much run everything, from the government to companies and organisations, including the FA, who are threatened by people like me. We don't fit their mould and, when we get into positions of authority, they're really not quite sure how to deal with us. Throughout the time I worked at the FA, they were legion.

On the positive side, there were many people at the FA who I have already talked about in this book who were inspirational, utterly supportive and a joy to work with. I will always remember their determination and hard graft, and their kindness towards me. But since the day I was sacked, I have never been back into the FA offices. I couldn't bear it. The wonderful Rachel Pavlou cleared my desk for me and that was that.

In my 15 years at the FA, I didn't ever want to build an empire. I wanted to build a structure. I didn't do this for the greater good of me – it was always for the betterment of women's football. I might be a control freak, but I am not an egotist.

The truth is that the FA got me on the cheap. They put me in charge of every level of the international pyramid of women's football at the FA – instead of paying for more staff to take responsibility for each of the levels. Not surprisingly, if you're put in charge of everything and you're determined that it'll succeed, then you'll gain a lot of control over the system. Ultimately, the powers that be at the FA didn't like that one little bit. I very much sensed that Alex Horne didn't want anyone within the women's game to have that amount of control ever again within the FA. So it's no surprise that I was sacked and cut off entirely from any future role. They wanted a new and totally fresh start, and that meant kicking me into touch.

Many of that management structure have now moved on, so I certainly would not rule out working for the FA again. After putting so much into developing the women's game in this country, it seemed nonsensical to airbrush me out of the FA's history. There's so much I am desperate to offer in terms of helping the women's game. Thankfully, UEFA and FIFA have offered me that opportunity, which has opened up a valuable new chapter in my life.

Chapter 18

FIFA

In the days after it became public that I'd been sacked as England manager, my phone rang constantly. I can't tell you how grateful I was to get such support and love from so many people I'd worked with over the years through the FA – as well as from major global figures in women's football, and footballing people from around the world.

I suppose proof of this came very soon after my sacking. I got a call from FIFA asking me to get more involved with their work globally. So, in February 2014, I flew over to FIFA headquarters in Zurich to discuss the details. In many ways this was my dream job. Travelling the world helping to develop the women's game. I know the high-ups at FIFA have been at the centre of controversy for a good while, and investigations into corruption within the organisation remain ongoing, but what I also know is that they do a great deal of valuable work around the world at grassroots and development level. This is what I really wanted to get involved with.

In October 2013, I was sent to South Korea to work on coaching development. From there, I went on to undertake under-17 technical study work in Bosnia, Azerbaijan, Slovenia and Norway, and it's been non-stop ever since. Alongside the work I've also been doing for UEFA, my work has taken me all around the world – to Canada, Finland, Kazakhstan, Serbia, Vietnam, Botswana, Switzerland, France, Germany, Poland, Cyprus, Malawi, Gibraltar, Namibia, Thailand, China, Belarus, Israel, Estonia, Malaysia, Gambia, Trinidad and Tobago, Jordan, Jamaica – and Bhutan.

I lead coaching courses around the world, to help develop and upskill coaches working in the women's game. Some countries I've visited, like South Korea, already have a fairly well-developed system and are looking for ways to get on to the next level. Others, like Malawi and Vietnam, are on the nursery slopes of developing and progressing women's football: they need a lot of help and advice in educating and growing their coaching structures.

I also act as a consultant for FIFA. I'm sent to assess the needs of individual countries by talking to everyone from their FA heads to coaches, managers and players. From there, I make a series of recommendations to the technical directors at FIFA. For example, after undertaking a consultation in Botswana, FIFA granted 250,000 euros to the country's FA to help them start building some decent infrastructure: some administrative offices to run the country's game from, and artificial pitches to play on. I felt proud that, in the position I'm now in, I could directly help make a difference there.

We moan about things here in the UK in terms of facilities, but in Malawi they play on pitches that are basically potholes with dust on top. And each 'pitch' can be home to ten or 12 different teams, so be constantly in use. It brought me back to my early playing days when we used to play on mud heaps and concrete. Similar to us way back then, the players in Malawi really have to learn good ball control because of the poor-quality surfaces. Resources were severely limited, but sometimes limitations can be liberations: FIFA money is now going into Malawi to help improve their situation and build a better footballing infrastructure.

Another important strand to my work with FIFA and UEFA is in technical observation. Basically, I am sent, along with half a dozen or so other highly qualified coaches, to forensically observe and assess individual international games and tournaments. I write a technical report highlighting the games' tactics, strategies, playing style, formations and so forth, and then deliver this back to FIFA and UEFA. It's all about looking at improving and advancing the game. From all of these results, I'm tasked with updating FIFA coaching manuals to highlight new advances and ideas that are emerging within the game – and old ones that are still working well at the highest level.

An important difference from my England travels is that, at last, I do get more time for sightseeing. Back in the day, all I saw was a hotel room, a training pitch and a football stadium. Now I'm enjoying being a tourist.

Trips to Jordan and Bhutan have resulted in the most culturally diverse experiences of my life – Jordan was one of my biggest challenges; Bhutan, one of my greatest joys. As soon as I arrived in Amman, I realised that my week of delivering a coaching course to Jordanian women would not be straightforward. In every other country I'd visited, the cohort of people selected to work with me were football coaches and players. In Jordan, my course consisted entirely of female PE teachers. They were all lovely women, but many of them didn't know much about football and its rules. A lot of them were not physically very fit and struggled to keep up with the different drills and exercises. To compound things, it was blisteringly hot throughout the week, the mercury hitting 38–40 degrees Celsius every day. This brought challenges for me. Just before I'd flown out to Jordan, I'd visited my doctor for a full body MOT. I'd been feeling rundown and put it down to the constant travelling. What the doc discovered was that my blood count was really low. Out on a training pitch under the beating sun every day drained me to the point of exhaustion. One day, I realised I was about to faint and ended the session early. The women on the course were complaining, too, about the heat and having to expend so much energy and bemoaning their general lack of football skills. It was the hardest course I'd ever delivered.

Being a woman in Jordan is very different from living in the UK. I always check with the administrators in each country I visit about any local dos and don'ts, customs or cultural habits. I am always aware, for example, that when delivering coaching courses in predominantly Muslim countries, it's vital to factor in breaks to allow for prayer time. As far as I humanly can, I try to adjust to and respect each new culture I work in.

But Jordan was hard. Men don't respect women out there, and that's very uncomfortable to be a part of. I got the smallest taste of it when I was at the reception counter in my hotel. I was talking to one of the receptionists when this guy stepped in front of me like I wasn't there. I very politely told him that I was being served, and he gave me a look of total shock. Like, 'A woman has just talked back to me!' He didn't quite know how to deal with it so just kept apologising.

From Jordan, it was immediately on to Bhutan, via an eight-hour plane journey to Bangkok, a five-hour flight to Guwahti in India, a 30-minute stopover, then a 35-minute hop, skip and a jump over the border to Bhutan's one and only international airport, Paro. Bhutan is a small, extremely mountainous, landlocked country squeezed between India and Tibet. Paro is located deep in a valley on the banks of a river and surrounded by mountains as high as 18,000 feet on either side. The experts consider it to be one of the world's most challenging airports – only eight pilots are certified to land at Paro, such is the difficulty of the landing, and they do it all manually. Landings and take-offs are only allowed during daylight hours and only under visual meteorological conditions. I mention all of this because of a secret I tried to keep from my England players for years.

Despite having more air miles than the head of the United Nations, I am utterly terrified of flying.

The nearest I came to absolutely losing it in front of the players was when we came home from the Euros in Finland in 2009. Our plane hit an air pocket, there was a loud bang and then the plane dropped like a stone. Poor Kelly Smith was flung off the toilet, and everyone around me was screaming. I dug my nails so hard into the arm of the guy sat next to me, it drew blood. Then the plane dropped again and there were more despairing screams. We eventually got home safely, but I was really shaken up.

I think I'm going to die every time I walk on to a plane. It hasn't been helped by a couple of other scary experiences over the years. Twice I've been on a plane that has come into land before suddenly pulling out and shooting back up into the sky again because parked planes were too near.

I never wanted the players to see me panicked and nervous before we even arrived somewhere to play a match. So I had to do something about it. I considered going on a fear of flying course but, in the end, I talked to Pippa about it, and she prescribed me diazepam. Now, I take it just before I get on a plane and it knocks me out nicely.

Not surprisingly, before the flight to Bhutan I was bricking it. For such a short flight, I'd chosen not to take the tablets, as I also wanted to see just how close we would come to the mountains.

But, happily, the pilot was so experienced, he immediately put my mind at rest. He described in great detail the approach we would take, how safe it would be and how many totally successful flights he'd personally taken into Paro. I was further put at ease when I realised the king's sister was sat two seats in front of me. The best of the eight pilots would surely have things well under control if a member of the local royalty was on board. I was so grateful to have made the flight. Because what I soon discovered was that Bhutan is an extraordinarily special place.

It's a strange mix of old and new, and East meets West. Bhutan didn't get television until 1999, but it's clearly had an effect on the younger generation, who are very Westernised – all baseball caps and r'n'b – whereas as the older generations continue to be very traditional in dress, customs and culture.

One of the direct effects of TV coming to Bhutan has been the growing popularity of football. Prior to television, the biggest participation sport in Bhutan was archery. But with satellite TV a window has opened into the world of top international league football, and the Bhutanese have liked what they've seen. A National Bhutan Premier League was set up for men, albeit with only six teams. They now have a national men's team, but it occupies the lowest FIFA ranking in the world.

If the men's game is underdeveloped in Bhutan, then women's football has barely started. There is no organised nationwide competition for women. They have a Bhutan women's national team, but it only plays sporadically, in friendlies against similarly small countries. Their first international game was held as recently as 2010.

But the exciting thing about Bhutan is its determination to develop football within its borders. The country already has a half-decent infrastructure, with a lot of football pitches and training facilities; the national stadium, which is also home to three of the men's National League Thimphu-based clubs, holds 25,000. The enthusiasm of the coaches and players I led a coaching course for was joyous. It was such a pleasure to spend a week working with such highly motivated and football-loving people, trying to improve their skills. They were desperate to learn.

Bhutan is a predominantly Buddhist country, and most people I met exuded a calm and peacefulness that was infectious. Family and community are deeply important to Bhutans, as is kindness to strangers. Throughout the week, I was treated with graciousness, good humour and respect. I was asked by the Bhutan FA if I'd consider coming back for three months to really kick-start their coaching plans. Perhaps not for now, but I never say never.

Being a Buddhist country, the people will do anything to avoid killing any living thing. The capital was full of wild dogs roaming the streets: they'd sit in the middle of the road, in among traffic, and roam freely – and because people weren't aggressive towards them, the dogs weren't aggressive either. Humans and hounds all just rubbed along together, pretty much ignoring one another. This laissez-faire attitude led to me witnessing one of the funniest things I have ever seen on a football pitch.

I was invited to the Changlimithang Stadium, home of the national side, to watch the end-of-season decider between the two top men's teams, Thimphu FC and Tertons. Bear in mind that the game was being shown live on TV in Bhutan. Midway through the first half, two wild dogs wandered on to the pitch. I was immediately expecting the referee to stop the game to get them off, but everyone ignored the duo. The hounds then wandered up the pitch into one of the penalty areas, right into the thick of the action. Again they were completely ignored, and the ball played around them. It soon became patently clear that one of the dogs was on heat … and there's no delicate way of putting this, but the two dogs started humping away on live TV. The game carried on, the dogs carried on. I couldn't believe what I was seeing. To everyone else, it was no big deal, just the norm.

Bhutan exemplified for me why I so enjoy my work with FIFA and UEFA: the opportunity to help make a difference, often in countries that are dirt poor and need help and support from outside to build an infrastructure for mass participation in football.

It took me a while to get used to working with interpreters, but when you don't speak a word of Thai, Polish, Korean or whatever, they're an invaluable asset. It can also be an unnerving exercise though: sometimes an interpreter has translated for me, and what I've seen is confused or worried looks on the faces of the local coaches and footballers. The interpretation and meaning of words can be very different in different languages, and a lot can be lost in translation. I now know to speak slowly, deliberately, and to use as many pauses as I can. Often I have to say the same thing four different ways for the interpretation to be correct.

Whenever I've led coaching sessions in English-speaking countries, I have always asked the coaches to imagine that they're working with footballers whose only language is Mandarin

Chinese. How do you get your ideas across to them? Well, obviously, not through words. For me, coaching is all about painting pictures: showing, not telling; practically demonstrating what you expect the coaches and players to do.

One of the most exciting things about the game of football is that it's a universal language. You could parachute a kid from Mongolia on to a football pitch in Spain, France, or wherever, and though that kid may not be able to speak a word of Spanish or French, if they play football, they'll absolutely understand everything that's happening on the pitch – because football is the number one global game, anyone who takes part anywhere in the world plays to the same rules. Though tactical formations may change, everyone knows what a goalie, a defender, a midfielder and an attacker does – that's why coaching is all about painting pictures; you don't necessarily need much, if any, language.

Look at men's and women's professional leagues around the world. There are Brazilians playing everywhere – from Russia and the Faroe Islands, to Japan and Korea; there are Serbians in Germany, Norway, Italy and Australia. The list goes on for ever. Yet when most of these players arrive at their new clubs, they don't speak a word of their new country's language. It certainly helps them socially and personally to learn more, but on the pitch football speaks a universal language.

It's been hugely exciting to work in so many different countries with so many different levels of player. From a coaching point of view, I've been able to apply what I already knew through experience. But I've also learnt a lot about new ways of communicating ideas in different cultures. More than anything, I am being paid to be an agent of change, and that I like very much.

Chapter 19

2015 and the World Cup

On International Women's Day 2015, FIFA launched its inaugural Women's Football and Leadership conference in Zurich. Experts and leaders from the game came together with representatives from business and industry to discuss ways to develop women's football and create more opportunities for women in leadership around the globe. I was honoured to be asked to make the keynote speech. I saw it as a great opportunity to air my feelings about something I have grave concerns over – to wit, how increasingly women coaches are being squeezed out of their own game.

I made the point that while increased interest in the sport may be welcome on many levels, its greater exposure has led to many more men wanting to coach and manage in the women's game. There is more kudos and money involved than ever before. This has led, across the globe, to a worrying trend of experienced, highly qualified women being replaced by much less qualified men. For example, Carolina Morace of Canada, Hesterine de Reus of Australia, Élisabeth Loisel of France and Vera Pauw of the Netherlands were all replaced by less experienced male coaches. I, too, of course, was replaced by Mark Sampson, and though personally I like the guy a lot there is no question that he is less experienced and less qualified than me. At the FA, under-17 manager Lois Fidler was also sacked and then replaced by a less qualified man. In our Women's Super League there is only one woman manager, Chelsea's Emma Hayes.

The added reason this is such a concern is that in both the men's and women's game there just aren't enough jobs to go around. It's a well-known fact that a high proportion of first-time professional managers never get a second job in the men's game. So as women's football becomes more of an attractive proposition, it does indeed provide an alternative opportunity for male managers.

Many people argue that the appointment of managers in the women's game shouldn't be about gender. It should be about who is best for the job. Fine. But if that's the case, why aren't women coaching and managing professional men's teams? There are a good number who are eminently well qualified and experienced enough to take on the jobs. So I'm afraid I find that a one-way argument. We need more women in the top jobs. With the women coaches we already have, we need opportunities for them to utilise their qualifications. Otherwise, what's the point?

In light of this, it was encouraging to see FIFA announce a quota system for women coaches ahead of the under-17 tournament in Jordan in 2016. Each country must include at least one woman coach and at least one woman medic, which sends out a strong signal to member countries – and, goodness knows, a lot of them need to hear it. Around the world, there are countries whose entire coaching and management teams of their women's sides are made up solely of men. Women must be given more encouragement to get involved in the game. Because once they're in, women are high achievers.

At the moment, though, only seven per cent of the world's coaches are women, which is a shocking statistic, especially when you consider that the past three Olympic gold medals and two out of the three most recent World Cups have been won by teams led by a female coach. At the 2015 World Cup only eight out of the 24 countries were managed by women.

And so to Canada, where I led a FIFA 12-day workshop for up and coming CONCACAF coaches in the women's game, from the Caribbean, USA and Canada. I'd met and worked with them all the year before at a series of workshops during the under-20 women's World Cup in Canada, and this was by way of a follow-up. Refreshingly, the majority of the participants were women. They were a bright bunch, too. Among their number was a marine biologist, a doctor and some university lecturers, and all of them were committed to spending their spare time learning as much as they could about coaching at all levels of the game. Some of them, undoubtedly, were aiming to switch careers and go full-time – so they were a well-motivated group to work with.

A year earlier I had given them all projects to work on, and the advances they'd made in their development through the 12 months was enormous. This is when you really get a buzz from the people you're working with. When they take the ball and run.

Helping me lead the workshops was former German goalie Silke Rottenberg, who's also Germany's current youth and under-20 teams' goalkeeping coach, and, for the first few days, former Mexican international Andrea Rodebaugh – both are fellow FIFA instructors. The aim was to help the further education of the 20 participants by taking them to a number of World Cup games and making detailed match analyses.

Together, we attended three games in Edmonton – the opener, Canada v China; Canada v New Zealand; and China v Netherlands

– and the coaches had to analyse and give a report on each of the games. Silke and I asked individuals to look at specific areas of each match, such as watching how the goalies dealt with crosses or back passes, or how the back four worked in relation to the attack. Then, afterwards, each coach would use this information as the basis of a coaching presentation they would deliver to the rest of the group.

It was a lot of fun to work with Silke, who is an old friend and a highly talented coach, and rewarding in the sense that you really felt like you were contributing towards making a change.

I was mega busy with the workshop for the first couple of weeks of the World Cup, but did manage to see England's quarter-final game against the hosts Canada in Vancouver. I sat in the stands next to my close friend, former Canada manager Carolina Morace, who'd been sacked in similar circumstances to me by the Canadian FA. Like me, she'd been an international player for her country, Italy, and went on to get all of her coaching badges.

Carolina is an amazing woman. She was an inspirational and unusual player. I remember once playing against her in an England v Italy international, and one of the Italian central defenders started to kick lumps out of one of our players. Carolina was always the fairest and most decent of footballers, but I was still amazed to see her grab her own teammate and start to kick the crap out of her. She bellowed swear words in Italian into the player's ear. Carolina was, and still is, a one-off.

We deliberately made sure we got seats together, because we wanted to share the experience. We kept whispering to one another, and wondered if we'd get caught on camera: we imagined commentators asking just what the two ex-managers of England and Canada were saying about the teams they used to coach and the way they were playing. What judgement they were

241

passing on the new managers. In truth, we were just having a giggle about them potentially asking those very questions on air.

You'd have to be made of stone not to have mixed feelings about watching a team you'd managed for 15 years turning out in the quarter-finals of a World Cup. Yes, it was strange not to be leading them out, but life moves on and you have to deal with it. I was really pleased for the girls that they made it through to the semis, beating the hosts 2–1. Pleased too for Mark Sampson. He'll have gained a lot of valuable experience from the Canada tournament. A lot of people were saying that I should take credit for England's good showing, but I wasn't about to. It was Mark's squad and he got them there through qualifying. Equally, if they'd done badly, I wouldn't have taken any of the blame either!

I was elated for the girls that they came away from the World Cup with a bronze medal each, and sincerely hope that England continue to progress. The girls were hard to beat, and I thought defended really well throughout the tournament. From what I saw, Laura Bassett showed what a strong personality she has and, with Steph Houghton, formed a really impressive defensive partnership. Claire Rafferty looked really sharp, and in midfield Fara Williams was her usual consistent self.

Would I want to manage an international team again? Since leaving the England job I've been offered four head coach jobs and turned them all down. Soon after getting the sack at the FA, I was asked to become the new manager of South Africa. But, in many ways, it was too soon after the sacking. And then in Canada, I was offered the vacant head coach's job of Nigeria. The Super Falcons won the first seven African championships, and their current aim is to make a mark on the world stage. They have some great young players coming through, evidenced in 2010 when they were runners-up in the under-20 women's World Cup to Silke Rottenberg's German side, narrowly losing 1–0. I think that once they gain more tactical know-how, Nigeria are potentially future World Cup winners.

I was approached by the president of the Nigerian FA, one of the country's greatest ever players, Mercy Akide. The idea was that I would be head coach, but also act as Mercy's mentor, so that they could bring her in as manager further down the line. They pretty much said I could name my own price. I thanked them very respectfully for their interest and went away to mull it over. I spoke to Michelle about it and we both agreed I had to say 'no'. Football is more than just a game. Not only are parts of Nigeria currently dangerous places, but a law that was passed there in 2014 became the bottom line for me not accepting the job. To quote from the legislation: 'Any person who registers, operates or participates in gay clubs, societies and organisations or directly or indirectly makes public show of same-sex amorous relationship in Nigeria commits an offence and shall each be liable on conviction to a term of ten years in prison.'

I could not work for any length of time in a country whose establishment holds such reactionary views about gay people. We may moan and complain about politicians here in the UK but, by and large, we are now all pretty much free to be who we want to be. I have all respect for Mercy and the Nigerian FA, but it had to be a 'no'.

So neither of those jobs were for me. Later, I was asked to manage Thailand and Trinidad and Tobago and turned them down too. Who knows what the future will bring? My philosophy has always been rule nothing in, rule nothing out. The wonderful thing about the past couple of years in my life has been that totally unexpected opportunities have come my way.

Soon after my return from the World Cup, I was off to Israel to work as a technical observer at the under-19 European Championships. Sweden won their second title at this level, beating Spain 3–1. It was exciting to watch the cream of Europe's young players, and there were some outstanding performances in Israel. As one of the technical observers, I had the honour of helping to choose the Squad of the Tournament. It gave an interesting pointer as to the direction in which European women's football may be going, in terms of which nations will dominate: the squad included four Spaniards, four Germans, three Swedes, three French, one Israeli and two English – goalie Caitlin Leach and midfielder Jodie Brett.

Now that I'm no longer at the FA, I find myself having the time and opportunity to involve myself in areas I would never have dreamt of. I went into Peterborough Prison with Ian Foster, who's now first team coach at Portsmouth, to do some coaching with the inmates. It was an experience I will definitely repeat. A number of the women were farting about and taking the mickey, so I found myself reading the riot act to them: 'You listen to what I say and you do what I say – otherwise you're back on the halls.' Then they were good as gold.

There wasn't exactly a lot of talent in there, but the girls were enthusiastic. Not surprisingly, they were loving being out of their cells and in the open air, and gave it their all. Well, apart from the regular occasions when they'd jog up to me and ask, 'Come on, Hope. Can't we have a fag break?' And I'd laugh and say, 'No, you bloody can't. You're here to play football!' Those girls gave me such a laugh. They were full of banter, cracking gags about how unfit they were and moaning about how hard I was pushing them. But they loved it, and so did I.

One very articulate woman was chatting to me and said she was at Loughborough University at the same time as Jane Ebbage, who became my coach at the Player Development Centre there. I said to her, 'What the hell are you doing in here?' She shrugged and replied that things had gone wrong for her. I know you're never meant to ask what anyone is in for, so I didn't.

I also have more time to reflect upon the women's game – to look at how things have changed, and what I would still like to see changed. It's clear there's been a slow revolution in the overall perception of the women's game in England. When I started playing, women footballers were regarded as weirdos, if they were regarded at all. There was no recognition that girls played football. We were largely invisible in the press and media. Even playing for England wasn't recognised at all. We paid to play, we trained no more than an hour and and a half a week. Qualified coaches were rare. We played in front of tiny crowds. With the best will in the world, it was totally amateurish.

Now we have central contracts for the national squad players. Many of the Women's Super League footballers earn a decent living wage and can just concentrate on playing football. Top players don't have to take on other jobs to get by. Sure, it's probably not even what a men's League Two player might earn, but it's progress.

In 2014–15, attendances at Women's Super League matches increased by more than 30 per cent on the previous season, with average gates of 728. That may not sound a lot, but when I used to play for Croydon in the mid-1990s we averaged less than a hundred fans a game.

The pyramid of our leagues now has a Women's Super League Division One and Two, with ten teams in each. A thriving FA Women's Premier League Northern Division and a Southern

Division. Beneath them are dozens more regional leagues up and down the country.

When the FA took over the running of the women's and girls' game in 1993, there were 11,200 registered players in England. Now, there are well over 200,000. That's a staggering increase. There are ever more women gaining coaching and refereeing qualifications. At the top of the professional tree it's now a commonplace that women officiate in the middle, and on the line in men's professional football. Though there are still some sexist dinosaurs around who give them plenty of stick, football fans in general are getting entirely used to women officiating matches and, rightly, have no problem with it. If they're good enough, it doesn't matter what gender they are.

Pioneering bodies like Women in Sport have relentlessly lobbied at the highest levels to gain more recognition, funding and profile for women's football, and fought to get more women involved in and engaged with sport. Now, it's an absolutely accepted commonplace that women and girls play football.

The increased media coverage has made a huge difference. When England got to the old World Cup final in 1995, we were lucky to get the odd one- or two-paragraph mention in the UK press. Twenty years on and England's exploits in the 2015 World Cup were front- and back-page news in all of the national newspapers. All the England games were televised live on mainstream BBC TV channels. The semi-final clash between England and Japan drew a peak BBC1 audience of 2.4 million, despite the kick-off time in the UK being midnight.

The internet and social media have had a hugely beneficial effect on helping to grow the game. Though Eni Aluko's experiences showed the downside of Twitter and the like, there are many pluses. I don't have any personal social media presence online, but that's because I don't want or need to. But when current players are in the spotlight, it's good that they have a way of communicating with their fans, and that there's a 'conversation' going on. After the 2015 World Cup, Eni had 42,000 Twitter followers, Casey Stoney 40,000.

Virtually all women's teams from the Super League down through the regional divisions now have their own very interactive websites, with extensive video highlights of games and chat forums. The inclusion of the England women's team on the *FIFA 16* video game is a huge step forward. Now football fans can play as England against 11 other international women's sides. Again, it's getting the game out there into the public consciousness.

When I was growing up, it was only possible to have professional male footballers as role models. That's changing fast, particularly since the 2015 World Cup and the increasing popularity of the Women's Super League. Young girls today have the likes of Fran Kirkby, Lucy Bronze and Toni Duggan on the back of their shirts, because they're so much more in the public eye.

With increased media profile, more big-hitting sponsorship has followed. The Women's Super League is sponsored by BT Sport, and more large companies are wanting to become involved in women's football. It's all a far cry from my early days at Millwall, when we struggled to get local firms to sponsor our boots and shinpads.

I'm proud to have played my part in helping change happen over the past 20 years. But there's still work to do. Globally, since I first became a player and then a manager, there's been a huge increase in the countries who've committed to trying to develop women's football. Around the world, more and more girls and women are getting involved in the game. One of my long-term aims is to help that revolution continue. I want to see more women coaches at the forefront of the game because, as I've argued, men still dominate the main roles across the women's international teams and domestic league. With all of the experiences I've had and the obstacles I've overcome, I'm in an ideal position to help more women gain the skills and the self-confidence to become leaders in the game. I am passionate about trying to give more women the opportunities that I had.

What are my hopes for the future? Tournament after tournament the coverage and exposure given to women's football in this country improves and, increasingly, more people get to see the game – but largely at tournament time. The exposure spikes every couple of years at the Euros and the World Cup, but then falls away. What we need is more coverage in between the major tournaments. It's great that BT are televising Women's Super League games, but a regular weekly presence on terrestrial TV would make a real difference. Perhaps a BBC *Match of the Day* for the WSL?

I like busy. And busy is what I continue to be, working principally for FIFA and UEFA. FIFA has tasked me with putting together a new world women's football manual, and I have a long calendar of coaching and football development visits to fulfil around the world. Beyond that, who knows what the next few years will bring for me?

In many parts of the world, women's fight against gender inequality is far more serious than just battling against conservative men in suits. In some countries, just gaining the right to play sports in male-dominated societies is a major issue for women. So there is still much work to be done, and I'm sure I will remain committed and involved in that, in whatever role.

Football *is* more than just a game. It can transform lives in so many ways. It fosters ideas of togetherness, community and responsibility for others. It offers the opportunity to strive, improve and aspire as an individual; to learn about discipline, determination and self-reliance. It can help change ideas and prejudice within societies. From me, all I can say is a big 'thank you' to the beautiful game. What would I have done without you?

Career Statistics
as England Manager

27 July 1998: England 0 Sweden 1, Friendly, Dagenham and Redbridge

15 August 1998: Norway 2 England 0, World Cup qualifier, Lillestrøm

13 September 1998: Romania 1 England 4, Qualification decider, Câmpina

11 October 1998: England 2 Romania 1, Qualification decider, Wycombe

26 May 1999: Italy 4 England 1, Friendly, Lugo

22 August 1999: Denmark 0 England 1, Friendly, Odense

15 September 1999: England 0 France 1, Friendly, Yeovil

16 October 1999: Switzerland 0 England 3, European qualifier, Zofingen

20 February 2000: England 2 Portugal 0, European qualifier, Barnsley

07 March 2000: England 0 Norway 3, European qualifier, Norwich

13 May 2000: England 1 Switzerland 0, European qualifier, Bristol

04 June 2000: Norway 8 England 0, European qualifier, Moss

14 August 2000: France 1 England 0, Friendly, Marseille

30 October 2000: Ukraine 1 England 2, European qualifier (play-off), Kiev

28 November 2000: England 2 Ukraine 0, European qualifier (play-off), Leyton Orient

22 March 2001: England 4 Spain 2, Friendly, Luton

27 May 2001: England 1 Scotland 0, Friendly, Bolton

24 June 2001: Russia 1 England 1, Euros 2001, Jena

27 June 2001: Sweden 4 England 1, Euros 2001, Jena

30 June 2001: Germany 3 England 0, Euros 2001, Jena

23 August 2001: England 0 Denmark 3, Friendly, Northampton

28 September 2001: Germany 3 England 0 World Cup qualifier, Kassel

04 November 2001: England 0 Holland 0 World Cup qualifier, Grimsby

24 November 2001: Portugal 1 England 1, World Cup qualifier, Gafanha da Nazaré

25 January 2002: Sweden 5 England 0, Friendly, La Manga

24 February 2002: England 3 Portugal 0 World Cup qualifier, Portsmouth

23 March 2002: Holland 1 England 4 World Cup qualifier, The Hague

04 September 2003: England 1 Australia 0, Friendly, Burnley

11 September 2003: Germany 4 England 0, Friendly, Darmstadt

25 September 2003: Italy 0 England 1 Friendly, Viareggio

21 October 2003: Russia 2 England 2, Friendly, Moscow

13 November 2003: England 5 Scotland 0, Friendly, Preston

19 February 2004: England 2 Denmark 0, Friendly, Portsmouth

22 April 2004: England 0 Nigeria 3, Friendly, Reading

14 May 2004: England 1 Iceland 0, Friendly, Peterborough

19 August 2004: England 1 Russia 2, Friendly, Bristol

18 September 2004: Holland 1 England 2, Friendly, Heerhugowaard

22 September 2004: Holland 0 England 1, Friendly, Tuitjenhorn

17 February 2005: England 4 Italy 1, Friendly, Milton Keynes

9 March 2005: Northern Ireland 0 England 4, Algarve Cup, Paderne

11 March 2005: Portugal 0 England 4, Algarve Cup, Faro

13 March 2005: England 5 Mexico 0, Algarve Cup, Lagos

15 March 2005: England 0 China 0, Algarve Cup, Guia

21 April 2005: England 2 Scotland 1, Friendly, Tranmere

06 May 2005: England 1 Norway 0, Friendly, Barnsley

26 May 2005: England 4 Czech Republic 1, Friendly, Walsall

05 June 2005: England 3 Finland 2, Euros 2005, Man City

08 June 2005: England 1 Denmark 2, Euros 2005, Blackburn

11 June 2005: England 0 Sweden 1, Euros 2005, Blackburn

01 September 2005: Austria 1 England 4, World Cup qualifier, Amstetten

27 October 2005: Hungary 0 England 13, World Cup qualifier, Tapolca

17 November 2005: Holland 0 England 1, World Cup qualifier, Zwolle

09 February 2006: Sweden 1 England 1, Friendly, Achna

09 March 2006: England 1 Iceland 0, Friendly, Norwich

26 March 2006: England 0 France 0, World Cup qualifier, Blackburn

20 April 2006: England 4 Austria 0, World Cup qualifier, Gillingham

31 August 2006: England 4 Holland 0, World Cup qualifier, Charlton

30 September 2006: France 1 England 1, World Cup qualifier, Rennes

25 October 2006: Germany 5 England 1, Friendly, Aalen

26 January 2007: China 2 England 0, China Cup, Guangdong

28 January 2007: USA 1 England 1, China Cup, Guangdong

30 January 2007: Germany 0 England 0, China Cup, Guangdong

03 March 2007: England 6 Russia 0, Friendly, Milton Keynes

11 March 2007: England 1 Scotland 0, Friendly, Wycombe

14 March 2007: England 0 Holland 1, Friendly, Swindon

13 May 2007: England 4 Northern Ireland 0, European qualifier, Gillingham

17 May 2007: England 4 Iceland 0, Friendly, Southend

11 September 2007: Japan 2 England 2, World Cup 2007, Shanghai

14 September 2007: Germany 0 England 0, World Cup 2007, Shanghai

17 September 2007: Argentina 1 England 6, World Cup 2007, Chengdu

22 September 2007: USA 3 England 0, World Cup 2007, Tianjin

27 October 2007: England 4 Belarus 0, European qualifier, Walsall

25 November 2007: England 1 Spain 0, European qualifier, Shrewsbury

12 February 2008: Sweden 2 England 0, Friendly, Larnaca

14 February 2008: Norway 1 England 2, Friendly, Larnaca

06 March 2008: Northern Ireland 0 England 2, European qualifier, Lurgan

20 March 2008: England 0 Czech Republic 0, European qualifier, Doncaster

08 May 2008: Belarus 1 England 6, European qualifier, Minsk

17 July 2008: Germany 3 England 0, Friendly, Unterhaching

28 September 2008: Czech Republic 1 England 5, European qualifier, Prague

02 October 2008: Spain 2 England 2, European qualifier, Zamora

09 February 2009: Finland 2 England 2, Friendly, Larnaca

11 February 2009: Finland 1 England 4, Friendly, Larnaca

05 March 2009: South Africa 0 England 6, Cyprus Cup, Larnaca

07 March 2009: France 2 England 2, Cyprus Cup, Larnaca

12 March 2009: Canada 1 England 3, Cyprus Cup, Larnaca

23 April 2009: England 3 Norway 0, Friendly, Shrewsbury

25 August 2009: Italy 2 England 1, Euros 2009, Lahti

28 August 2009: Russia 2 England 3, Euros 2009, Helsinki

31 August 2009: Sweden 1 England 1, Euros 2009, Turku

03 September 2009: Finland 2 England 3, Euros 2009, Turku

06 September 2009: Holland 1 England 2, Euros 2009, Tampere

10 September 2009: Germany 6 England 2, Euros 2009, Helsinki

25 October 2009: England 8 Malta 0, World Cup qualifier, Blackpool

26 November 2009: Turkey 0 England 3, World Cup qualifier, İzmir

24 February 2010: England 1 South Africa 0, Cyprus Cup, Larnaca

27 February 2010: England 0 Canada 1, Cyprus Cup, Larnaca

01 March 2010: Switzerland 2 England 2, Cyprus Cup, Larnaca

03 March 2010: Italy 2 England 3, Cyprus Cup, Larnaca

25 March 2010: England 3 Austria 0, World Cup qualifier, QPR

01 April 2010: England 1 Spain 0, World Cup qualifier, Millwall

20 May 2010: Malta 0 England 6, World Cup qualifier, Ta' Qali

19 June 2010: Spain 2 England 2, World Cup qualifier, Aranda de Duero

29 July 2010: England 3 Turkey 0, World Cup qualifier, Walsall

21 August 2010: Austria 0 England 4, World Cup qualifier, Krems

12 September 2010: England 2 Switzerland 0, World Cup qualifier (play-off), Shrewsbury

16 September 2010: Switzerland 2 England 3, World Cup qualifier (play-off), Wohlen

19 October 2010: South Korea, 0 England 0, Peace Cup, Suwon

21 October 2010: New Zealand 0 England 0, Peace Cup, Suwon

02 March 2011: Italy 2 England 0, Cyprus Cup, Larnaca

07 March 2011: Canada 2 England 0, Cyprus Cup, Nicosia

09 March 2011: South Korea 0 England 2, Cyprus Cup, Larnaca

02 April 2011: England 2 USA 1, Friendly, Leyton Orient

17 May 2011: England 2 Sweden 0, Friendly, Oxford

27 June 2011: Mexico 1 England 1, World Cup 2011, Wolfsburg

01 July 2011: New Zealand 1 England 2, World Cup 2011, Dresden

05 July 2011: Japan 0 England 2, World Cup 2011, Augsburg

09 July 2011: France 1 England 1 (England lost 4–3 on pens), Leverkusen

17 September 2011: Serbia 2 England 2, European qualifier, Belgrade

22 September 2011: England 4 Slovenia 0, European qualifier, Swindon

27 October 2011: Holland 0 England 0, European qualifier, Zwolle

23 November 2011: England 2 Serbia 0 European qualifier, Doncaster

28 February 2012: Finland 1 England 3, Cyprus Cup, Nicosia

01 March 2012: Switzerland 0 England 1, Cyprus Cup, Achna

04 March 2012: France 3 England 0, Cyprus Cup, Larnaca

06 March 2012: England 1 Italy 3, Cyprus Cup, Paralimni

31 March 2012: Croatia 0 England 6, European qualifier, Vrbovec

17 June 2012: England 1 Holland 0, European qualifier, Manchester

21 June 2012: Slovenia 0 England 4, European qualifier, Velenje

19 September 2012: England 3 Croatia 0, European qualifier, Walsall

20 October 2012: France 2 England 2, Friendly, Paris

06 March 2013: England 4 Italy 2, Cyprus Cup, Nicosia

08 March 2013: Scotland 4 England 4, Cyprus Cup, Nicosia

11 March 2013: England 3 New Zealand 1, Cyprus Cup, Nicosia

13 March 2013: England 1 Canada 0, Friendly, Rotherham

07 April 2013: England 1 Canada 0, Friendly, Rotherham

26 June 2013: England 1 Japan 1, Friendly, Burton upon Trent

04 July 2013: Sweden 4 England 1, Friendly, Ljungskile

12 July 2013: England 2 Spain 3, Euros 2013, Linköping

15 July 2013: England 1 Russia 1, Euros 2013, Linköping

18 July 2013: France 3 England 0, Euros 2013, Linköping

Acknowledgements

There are so many people who have been part of my life in football and the journey I have taken. A big thanks all round, and, if for some reason you are omitted from this text of thanks, you know you are a part of my story.

Firstly I must say thanks to the FA, to Howard Wilkinson, Robin Russell and Kelly Simmons for believing I could do the job as England manager.

To my mum, my brother Brian and my sister-in-law Gill, thank you for supporting me regardless and believing in my ambitions.

To Michelle – 'forever the positive' – who gave me the confidence and made me believe anything I want to achieve is possible. For her unconditional love for all these years.

Brenda and Beth, who have always been there and encouraged me (told me) to start my journey and believing in my ambitions.

To Angie Gallimore – you are special!

To the wonderful Marcia Wilson, Mandy Croston and Misia Gerviz for your friendship and support.

To all the staff I worked with over the years who were all part of making the England teams greater, and who all remain my good friends today: Paul Smalley, Steve Rutter, Perry Suckling, Brent Hills, Keith Rees, Mark Phillips, Graham Keeley, Pippa Bennett, Mary Dowd, Charlotte Cowie, Dawn Scott, Naomi

Datson, Louise Fawcett, Tracey Kevins, Jill Chapman, Yvonne McLaughlin, Sigrid Baumman, Phil Worrall, Dave Lee (Daisy), Mo Marley, Lois Fidler, Kay Cossington, Ronald Thompson (thanks, Cuz), Colin (Mr) Norman, Margaret McGough, Ros Potts, Donna McIvor, Helen Croft, Lucy Wellings, Kelly Simmons, Helen Nicolaou, Caroline Clay, Graeme Bowerbank, Lucia Sanchez, Katherine Knight, Bev Ward, Morag Taylor, Alex Stone, Glenn Lavery, Scott Field, Stuart Mawhinney, Johan, Andy Carter, Tom Holder, Jag Chagger.

To all the players I worked with over the years – it was truly a privilege!

Special thanks to Mr May (Alan), my adopted dad! Thanks for your continued guidance, support, advice and love – forever taking the time to listen; always there when needed and undoubtedly always will be.

Dear Rachel Pavlou … you are special. My co-pilot and good friend for so many years. Thank you, thank you.

Charlotte. Thank you for believing in this book … I look forward to that drink.

And finally, to you, Marvin … it has been truly special. Thank you for your patience. And for your hours of time and dedication in pulling this project together. Well done! In you I have also found a friend.

Index